LESSONS IN LOVE

TO BOOST

YOUR MARRIAGE

By Remi Alaka

Remi Alaka
LESSONS IN LOVE TO BOOST YOUR MARRIAGE

Copyright © 2021 Remi Alaka
ISBN 979-8736-1279-79

Cover and interior design by Golden Truth Publishing
Kyiv, Ukraine. All rights reserved.
www.goldentruth.pro

Dedicated to the love of my life, my beautiful wife and best friend. You mean the world to me. Thank you for leading me to Christ. I appreciate your example of a God-fearing wife.

Acknowledgement

This book has been the child of my brain, but it has been a long time coming. It is something I have conceived for a very long time, so it is great to finally see it in print.

As a result, I have so many people to thank:

The clients Helen and I have had the privilege to coach.

My wife and best friend – Helen, who read the 'raw' draft of each lesson and picked out the things that needed to be repositioned. Without her help, support and encouragement, this book would not have been written. So, I am immensely grateful for her support.

Special thanks to my son, James. When he read the first chapter and volunteered to write the forward, it saved me a lot of aggro in looking for someone else to fill the role. I really appreciate his contributions in reviewing lesson one.

I am particularly grateful for the constructive feedback and comments on the manuscript from the following people: Marvin Antah, Morris Ximenes, Ben and Ronke Kokoruwe, Mike and Joanne Farrell, Iain Williams, James Thomas and Mike Desouza.

I am enormously grateful for the guidance and sound advice from Randal Porter, my mentor in the final stages of this project.

Without all these people, the book would still remain as a conceived idea. It just shows that we all need support from each other for anything to blossom from conception to delivery. I am grateful for every one of you. May God bless you richly.

Contents

Acknowledgement   4

Foreword   8

Preface   12

Introduction   14

Lesson One: Laying the Foundation
of a Great Marriage   17

Lesson Two: Communication -
From the Heart   35

Lesson Three: Resolving Quarrels
in Marriage   55

Lesson Four: Dealing With Hurts   75

Lesson Five: Unity in Marriage   103

Final Words From Me   121

References   123

FOREWORD

My father has always been a superhero to me. From as early as I can remember, he has been a friend, a disciplinarian, a teacher, and a coach, but most importantly, he has showed me unconditional love and support through everything. He has also made sure that honest and open channels of communication exist within our family unit. However, before Dad came to Christ, there was another side to him. I was shocked to learn that my Dad's sacrificial nature was not always his temperament, and his attitude was usually selfish due to a different perspective.

Nonetheless, after his encounter with Christ and transformation as a result, his mindset and family values totally changed. He attributes everything good in his life to his love for God, his family, and his constant yearning for more biblical knowledge; It is evident to me that his application of biblical principles in relation to his personal life, his marriage, his parenting, his friendships, and his professional life have made him into the kind-hearted person he is today. I am grateful that I had him as a role model growing up, even if I was not always aware of how lucky my brothers and I were to have him leading our household.

I also didn't realise that my parents' marriage was special until I entered my teenage years, started dating myself, and became aware of the many dysfunctional relationships that surrounded me on any given day. It was a sharp realisation to discover at fifteen that not every husband and wife talked through their issues to prevent the harbouring of resentment. Whilst I knew that not every couple was biblically-inclined, I didn't know that couples who were spiritual, religious, or in touch with God and the Bible, didn't always see eye-to-eye, or even care to remedy that issue! Until then, I hadn't realised that not all married couples refrain from using hurtful language toward one another. It never occurred to me that it wasn't a given for a marriage to be harmonious, full of love, and continually growing, year after year. Until then, my parents' relationship never seemed special because it was all I knew, and all I was exposed to. I thought, naively I must add, that every child with married parents benefitted from the same example of love and devotion that my mother and father displayed to each other on a daily basis.

Now, as a married man, I appreciate the bond between my parents even more. I am so grateful that they are always approaching situations with love, and I am thankful for witnessing them communicate successfully, watching them listen with the intent to understand, rather than listen with the intent to reply. I have asked them for advice, and will continue to do so for the duration of my marriage. I am indebted to God that he blessed my brothers and I with parents who are willing to unlearn things detrimental to their character, and who constantly search for new ways to become better people, parents, spouses, friends, and servants to God.

When I lived at home, it was not uncommon for me to see my parents host couples and go through marriage counselling with them, spending hours poring over books and engaging in enriching and enlightening conversation. I also cannot count the number of times I have had couples, and individuals, express the same sentiment to me: that my parents helped them understand their duties in a relationship better, and that they are great role models.

This book is a labour of love. Dad has spoken about wanting to put some of the lessons he has learned throughout his life on paper for many years, although he found it hard to find the time to start. I haven't asked him, but I am sure self-doubt often proved a barrier, or even provided a ready-made excuse for him not to convert his thoughts to ink. Nonetheless, he overcame whatever had prevented him from beginning his journey as an author.

Writing is difficult. It is a daunting task for anybody, specifically for someone like my father, who openly admits that reading and writing are not his strongest skills. That's what makes this body of work even more special in my eyes. My dad understands that he has been blessed with nuggets of knowledge that could potentially help ailing marriages, and he cast aside his own fears in order to share them with you, the reader, in hope that you will gain something that can enrich your lives as well.

I could fill a book with all the things I admire about Remi Alaka, or with how grateful I am to have the parents I have. But this isn't my work, so I do not want to take too much of your time with my thoughts as I am sure you are eager to get started! However, I will leave you with this parting thought: for over thirty years, I have watched my parents grow more in love every day, which is no easy feat. Please open your hearts while you make your way through this book, as these **Lessons in Love** can truly become the blueprint to creating a fruitful marriage.

By James Alaka

PREFACE

After being told "...you may now kiss the bride", walking down the aisle, and returning from your honeymoon, the reality of marriage starts to set in. Whether, you and your spouse dream of living in a mansion, having multiple kids, or starting a business together, the hope is that you enjoy a long and fruitful union together.

Everybody plans for their marriage to be successful; we do not plan for it to be bad, but what do we do when our marriage does not turn out the way we had imagined? Every married couple envisions a great relationship when they say their vows, so how should we react when the reality of marriage isn't matching what we planned?

You have to be brave to start a marriage. God created man and woman with the intention of them joining in marriage. However, in **1 Corinthians 7:28**, Paul, in addressing this issue with the Church in Corinth said, "*...those who marry will face many troubles in this life and I want to spare you of this*". The only way we can avoid the troubles in marriage, based on my life experience and my experience working with other couples, **is to follow God's plan for marriage as laid out in the Bible**. Any other way will only present a temporary solution.

Are you looking for a temporary fix to the problems in your marriage or are you looking for a lasting solution?

Most people I know, including those my wife and I have worked with, are looking for a lasting solution to the problems that surface in their marriage, but they are not willing to put in the effort, or make the necessary sacrifices, to make their marriage work, which is a pity!

Are you willing to put in the effort and make sacrifices to make your marriage work?

Your answer to this question is pertinent to how much you'll get out of this book.

Be sure of this, you will get back from your marriage, the investment – in terms of effort, care and attention - you put into it.

I believe you have this book in your hand because you are committed to working on your marriage, to make it the best it can be and bring glory to God, or you want to use the lessons to help someone else have a fruitful marriage.

Biblical principles are ideal for Christian marriages, but they will only work for those who implement them **wholeheartedly**.

INTRODUCTION

Who is this book for?

This book is written for married couples who want to boost the quality of their marriage, irrespective of their religious persuasion. Whether you have recently got married or are seasoned married couples, there is something in the book for everyone. The definition of marriage adopted in this book is a union between a biological man and a biological woman.

The principles in the book will be helpful in guiding readers to identify issues that cause unhappiness in their marriage and how to overcome them.

Although there are references to Bible passages, this is deliberate because as a Christian Marriage Coach, I find the Bible relevant to the work I do. The application of biblical principles changed my life and my marriage; in fact, it changed everything about me for the better.

From a position of living a self-centred life to living a life considering the needs of my wife above mine is more fulfilling and rewarding. By extension, biblical principles have also helped me in other areas of my relationship with friends, colleagues and family members.

It is interesting when my wife and I meet non-church goers for the first marriage coaching session and ask them why they chose to have us help them with issues in their marriage. The common answer we get is that they have heard about us from their friends or relatives and they know we will be objective and impartial in supporting them.

We are yet to come across a non-religious couple who has declined our help when we tell them we will refer to the Bible.

After all, when you employ the services of a workman to carry out work on your property, you will expect them to do their job with the best tools available to them. Similarly, the best tool available to Helen and I is the Bible.

Lesson One offers the readers eight biblical principles we have found helpful to us and helpful to couples we have worked with over the years, which will work for you if you and your spouse commit to them and apply them to your marriage on a consistent basis. There is no room for complacency when it comes to applying these principles to your marriage.

Lesson Two is about communication; an essential 'commodity' in the world we live in. When communication breaks down between two countries, it leads to war. Similarly, when it breaks down in a household, it leads to all sorts of ill feelings towards each other. This section will explore the levels of a couple's communication. Just as a swimming pool has a shallow and a deep end, couples can communicate at a shallow or a deep level. You will be asked to evaluate the level you communicate at, and you will also find practical suggestions on how to connect with each other and communicate at a deep level.

Lesson Three addresses the causes of quarrels in a marriage and suggests solutions to minimise them when they occur. Because of the differences in couple's upbringing and the differences in their perspective, disagreements are inevitable in a marriage, but they must be addressed sooner rather than later. This lesson also covers the benefits of addressing quarrels in time and the consequences of not addressing them in time.

Lesson Four is about dealing with hurts. Even in the most loving relationships, married couples hurt each other intentionally or unintentionally. This lesson will help you to understand how your spouse feels when you hurt them and how you should respond to their feelings. You will also find the idea of radical forgiveness in this lesson.

Lesson Five introduces the idea of unity in marriage. It is vital that married couples are united in their thinking and approach to 'doing' marriage. A house divided against itself cannot stand. Marriage is complex because it brings two people from different backgrounds, culture or perspectives together under one roof, with the aim of loving and caring for one another. This is a challenging task for most couples, so this lesson will help you to understand that unity with the creator first is key, and how couples can be united with each other.

There are various exercises embedded in the lessons, and further questions at the end of each lesson. To get maximum benefit from these exercises, I would encourage you to schedule a time of reflection to answer the questions and a time of coming together to discuss before moving on to the next lesson.

Lesson One

Laying the Foundation of a Great Marriage

In this lesson, I will begin by presenting eight biblical qualities my wife and I have found instrumental in our own marriage and helpful to couples who want to have a great marriage. I pray that they will help you as well.

The foundation of any given building will determine how well it stands up against the elements; storms and floods included. I once observed a construction company putting up a structure near my office in Twickenham, London, United Kingdom. It took them three months to lay the foundation and a further six months to build the entire eight storey building! For those in the construction industry, it is obvious why they had to spend a considerable amount of time on the foundation - to make sure it is solid; a deeper foundation translates to a more sturdy and dependable base structure.

Similarly, it is important that the foundation of a great marriage is solid. Like a building in times of adverse conditions, all marriages will go through their stormy periods where they are hit with things determined to break them. From my experience, those marriages where the husband and wife have agreed to put biblical principles into practice, will survive.

As Jesus said in **Matthew 7:24-27** *"Therefore, everyone who hears these words of mine and puts them into practice is like a wise man who built his house on the rock. The rain came down, the streams rose, and the winds blew and beat against that house, yet it did not fall, because it had its foundation on the rock. But everyone who hears these words of mine and does not put them into practice is like a foolish man who built his house on sand. The rain came down, the streams rose, and the winds blew and beat against that house, and it fell with a great crash."*

The foundation of a marriage will determine its quality. Implementing biblical principles will work best when the two of you are committed to applying them to your relationship.

The principles we found helpful in our marriage, which we recommend to married couples, are:

1. True Friendship

My father used to say many times that "a friend in need is a friend indeed". Another of his famous saying is "show me your friend and I will tell you who you are." As a young boy, I really didn't fully understand what these sayings meant, but as I grew up, I understood. When I look back at my life and the people I could call true friends, they are few in number. At one point in my life, I had a lot of friends, but I cannot say that all of them were true friends. This made me conclude that a true friend is one that sticks by you at all time. Someone you can share your secrets with, be open and honest with and will accept you for who you are. Someone who makes you feel happy when you are in their company.

In **John 15:15**, Jesus said to his followers: *"I no longer call you servants, because a servant does not know his master's business. Instead, I have called you friends, for everything that I learned from my father I have made known to you"*

Jesus gave everything to his friends – his knowledge of God and his own life, for example. He is our model for friendship, because he loved without limits, and he did not withhold anything from his friends. He shared his life with them freely. They knew his mission - to seek and save the lost *(Luke 19:10)* and that one day, he will give his life as a ransom for many *(Matthew 20:28)*. Jesus' friends were not in the dark about his life.

By the same token, **your spouse should not be in the dark about your life.** I will encourage you to make everything about your life known to each other. If your spouse asks you anything about your life, it is best to be honest in your reply; it will draw you closer to each other and ensure that a bond built around trust and friendship becomes a pillar in your relationship.

Is there anything you are holding back from your spouse? It is not worth it, be open with your true friend.

For some people, the idea of being completely open and honest might be challenging as there are things in their past they are embarrassed to discuss.

> **Is there anything you are holding back from your spouse? It is not worth it, be open with your true friend.**

However, if they are affecting the relationship between you and your spouse, I would encourage you to get help and resolve to share them. Consequently, you can then liberate yourself from the things stopping you from building a true friendship with your spouse. Total transparency will ultimately bring you closer to one another.

Further questions to consider:

- How much do you value the friendship between you and your spouse?
- Discuss how you can enhance it.
- List and discuss the barriers preventing you as a couple from having a true friendship.
- What are the benefits of letting your spouse know everything about you?

---

2. Communication

The way some couples communicate with one another leaves a lot to be desired. The tongue can be destructive and the words that escape our mouths can have a damaging effect on people's lives and self-esteem. The Bible says in **James 3:8**

"But no human being can tame the tongue. It is a restless evil, full of deadly poison."

The tongue has something mortal about it, for it produces a kind of death. Its deadly poison fills its venom in relationships with slander, malice, anger, and envy. Verbal malice **destroys** the reputation of men, women, leaders, and churches.

James does not mean that the tongue is impossible to tame, but is something extremely **difficult** to control. It will take the power of God to tame it.

The words that come out of our mouths are powerful; they can build people up or destroy them.

It is shameful to hear some of the hurtful words couples sometimes throw at each other when they are arguing.

The people in the two examples below are fictitious, but the words they say are true, as my wife and I have heard, more times than we'd like to say, from couples we have mentored in the past.

Ann said, *"my husband speaks to me as if I am a child with no brain, and it is hurtful and makes me lose confidence in my ability to do anything with my life."*

Anthony said, *"my wife has a tongue as sharp as a razor. The words she uses when we are arguing cut so deep and make me feel small."*

Are you like Ann or Anthony?

The Bible tells us in **Ephesians 4:29:** *'Do not let any unwholesome talk come out of your mouths, but only what is* *helpful for building others up according to their needs, that it may benefit those who listen'.*

Unwholesome talk is belittling and makes one partner feel inferior and insecure in the relationship, so try to be mindful of how your behaviour affects your spouse.

Some things used to belittle people are:

- Name calling
- Swear/Curse words
- Statements alluding to a lack of sense or intelligence
- Devaluing one's work ethic
- Negative comments - and undermining words and actions

The damage done by these things cannot be easily undone, even if you follow them up with positive words. Human nature dictates that people generally tend to focus more on the negative rather than positive.

For example, it is common for some people who were belittled by their parents as children to carry that trauma into adulthood, and marry someone who displays the same toxic behaviour.

I would encourage you to stop this behaviour, if the above describes you, as it hinders your marriage and makes your spouse miserable. This may have an irreversible effect on you both.

To avoid inadvertently belittling your spouse, you should make a conscious effort to remove negative words from your vocabulary and encourage your spouse daily. It does not cost anything to say something nice to your best friend and life partner on a daily basis.

Further questions to consider:

- Do you communicate better with work colleagues than you do with your spouse?

- If your answer to the question above is yes, is it the case of familiarity breeds contempt? Discuss how you can improve communication between you and your spouse.

- Does your spouse know your hang ups about communication? If not, make time to discuss these as they will improve communication between you.

- If you were belittled by your parents or significant others, how much of that is affecting how you communicate with your spouse?

---

3. Prayer

James 5:16 reads: *"...Pray for each other so that you may be healed"*.

Praying for and with one another shows that you care about each other's wellbeing. Taking your situations to God, who knows both of you better than you know yourselves, is the best thing you can do for your marriage. Over the years of working with couples, my wife and I have noticed that couples who pray together grow in their relationship with God, and ultimately, they grow closer to each other.

Mr and Mrs A have a hectic schedule with work and home life, but they made the decision to pray every day, either at the beginning of the day (early mornings) or at night before bedtime. During their prayer time, they present their requests to God.

Prayer can act as a therapeutic activity that strengthens the foundations of your marriage, and calms your spouse and your troubles. After all, committing your worries, fears, struggles, and stresses to God will alleviate tension in you, your partner and your marriage; tension you may not have noticed. Remember what Peter said about Jesus in **1 Peter 5:7:** *"Cast all your anxieties on him because he cares for you."* I find that connecting with Jesus in prayer helps to reduce my anxieties, burdens and stresses.

If you are a couple who believes in the Bible, do you pray together? If not, why not?

Tips – make time to regularly pray together, and talk through your prayer needs to encourage vulnerability and togetherness.

Further questions to consider:

- Are you open and honest when you pray with your spouse?

- What barriers do you need to address to get into a habit of regular prayer with your spouse?

- Is your spouse aware of your spiritual, emotional, psychological and sexual struggles?

- Do you believe that praying together is inviting God to intervene in your marriage?

4. Humility

Being humble is a character trait that isn't championed in today's society. The fast-paced nature of the modern world tends to focus more on brash, outlandish and often ruthless behaviour; with many of the prominent figures in entertainment, sports, and the corporate world displaying a marked lack of humility.

1 Peter 5:5 says *"All of you, clothe yourselves with humility toward one another, because, God opposes the proud but shows favour to the humble"*

A humble person will display qualities such as: talking less and listening more, choosing to be at peace instead of being right, and showing modesty in all aspects of life.

If you and your spouse aim to be the first to say, "I am sorry", you are more likely to have a good marriage. However, it is more than just saying sorry, you should mean it. Also, you should be able to view things from your spouse's perspective; this in itself shows humility and will show your partner that you are not only humble, but care about how they are thinking and feeling.

The opposite of humility is pride. In my experience, most proud people do not admit that they have contributed to the issues causing problems in their marriage. They make it look like it is their spouse's fault, even when the evidence is stacked against them. They often find a way to explain themselves and shift the blame onto their spouse, but this behaviour is damaging to a marriage.

If you are not sure whether you are a proud person, ask people who really care about you to give you their honest opinion of you. Then, consider how your pride is affecting your spouse's well-being and make the decision to change your attitude.

Further questions to consider:

- How will your friends / spouse / children / work colleagues / church members / neighbours describe you? A proud or humble person?

- Can you identify instances when you could have shown humility towards your spouse? What specific areas need change and/or growth?

- Discuss with your spouse the benefits of practising humility towards each other in your relationship.

---

5. Encouragement

Being told positive things about yourself almost always generates a good feeling. Encouragement from somebody you love feels even better. A passage from **1 Thessalonians 5:11**: *'Therefore encourage one another and build each other up, just as in fact you are doing'*.

The Oxford Dictionary definition of encouragement is as follows: *"to give support, confidence or hope to someone..."*

Your spouse needs you the most when they are going through challenges in their life. Challenges can cover a myriad of issues; some that we have encountered are health problems, family issues, bereavement, job loss and the menopause.

Supporting your spouse at the time they most need it will lift their spirits and enhance the quality of your relationship. Most people I know who are of a similar age to me grew up in homes where they were given little to no encouragement, and as a result, they are always looking for encouragement and words of affirmation from other people around them as a surety that they are doing okay. I can hardly remember receiving encouragement from my parents or significant others when growing up and I am one of those who thrive on it. It spurs me on to greater heights when it comes from people who really care about me.

> Your spouse will appreciate words of encouragement from you all the time, but especially during difficult times.

Remind your spouse why they are so special to you. Commend them on their successful endeavours. Comfort them with reassurance when they are feeling low. **Your spouse will appreciate words of encouragement from you all the time, but especially during difficult times.**

How often do you encourage your spouse?

From the moment I discovered that daily encouragement adds some spice to my relationship with Helen, I strive to do it daily, and sincerely from the heart. Whether it is complimenting her beauty, her ability to manage our finances efficiently, which has kept us in the black for the past 10 years, to her creative cooking exploits.

The rule for me is to look for any small or big thing she does or endures that I admire about her. As I write this book, she is going through intense shoulder pain caused by frozen shoulder. We are awaiting a date for her to have surgery. But she has been managing it incredibly well. On top of that, she is also going through various health challenges that causes pain on other parts of her body. However, I have never heard her complain about these pains, she just gets on with whatever she has to do. As a loving husband, I can only encourage and compliment her on how she is comporting herself through these challenges.

Your spouse may do many good things for you, your family, his or her employer / employees, in the community you live in, so if you open your eyes wide, you will see that they deserve encouraging words. So, get into the habit of encouraging your spouse today. You will see the benefits of doing this in your relationship. However, a word of caution: remember that it must be done with sincerity and from the heart. Do not be flippant when doing this.

You can encourage and compliment verbally, by writing them a card, by cooking a special dish or buying them a gift. You can also be creative about how you do it as you know your spouse better than anyone else.

> **Further questions to consider:**
>
> - How do you want your spouse to support you when you are going through challenges? Remember, few people are good at mind reading – your spouse may not be one of them. More about this in chapter two.
>
> - How often do you tell your spouse how special they are to you?
>
> - If encouraging your spouse is not a natural thing to you, are you willing to learn how to do it? If yes, make a concerted effort to look out for anything positive your spouse does, take notes and use them to encourage him/her, when they are not expecting it.

6. Honesty

The two passages succinctly state my views on honesty in a relationship. **Ephesians 4:25:** *"Therefore, each of you must put off falsehood and speak truthfully to your neighbour."* (in this case – your spouse) and **Colossians 3:9:** *"Do not lie to one each other since you have taken off your old self with its practises."*

It is good to be truthful with your spouse ALL OF THE TIME, even if you do not entirely agree with their point of view.

However, remember that this ought to be done with the utmost love and respect, otherwise it will not be well-received. Being truthful will allow for constructive discourse between your partner and yourself to develop. **Once you have established communication permeated with love, you will find that being honest with one another no longer feels like a burden or chore.**

Honesty is the wisest path. So, begin with a commitment to being honest with one another. Start today. Honesty builds trust and deeper togetherness.

> Once you have established communication permeated with love, you will find that being honest with one another no longer feels like a burden or chore.

Dishonesty on the other hand, widens the emotional gap between you and your spouse. If you desire to be close to your spouse, I advise that total honesty should be treasured by you and your spouse. This may be difficult for some people to comprehend, but trust me, when you start to practise it, you will notice the difference it makes to your relationship and your self-worth.

Consider how you can demonstrate to your spouse that you value honesty in your marriage.

Further questions to consider:

- If you have not been honest with your spouse, what is stopping you from starting to be honest today?

- Is being honest with your spouse feel burdensome to you? If yes, I encourage you to get help.

- What falsehood do you need to get rid of so you can be closer to your spouse?

---

7. Kiss of Love

1 Peter 5:14 says, *"Greet one another with a kiss of love..."* If this were important enough to remind the first century church members, how much more important do you think this must be in a marriage?

Kissing your spouse is a simple romantic gesture that can instantly change one's mood. The symbolism associated with kissing is also not lost on me, as it can be used as a reminder of when you kissed on your wedding day for the first time as Husband and Wife; a day filled with happy memories that personify your joint ambition as a couple and your commitment to support each other for eternity.

In his article titled *"The Surprising Benefits of Kissing"*, Sean Horan stated: Kissing is important in your marriage as it increases your self-esteem by making you feel appreciated and helps your state of mind.

How often do you kiss your spouse? If not daily, why? A simple gesture like a kiss or a hug can sometimes express a feeling we cannot put into words.

Further questions to consider:

- Do you only kiss your spouse when you want something from them?
- Is kissing your spouse a chore to you? If so, why?
- What is acting as a barrier to show mutual affection towards each other?

8. Sexual Intimacy

A verse I often refer to regarding sexual intimacy can be found in **1 Corinthians 7:5:** *'Do not deprive each other [of sexual intimacy] except perhaps by mutual consent...'*

Sexual temptations are difficult to withstand because they appeal to the natural desires God has given us, but marriage provides God's way to satisfy these desires and to protect both of you against temptation.

Married couples have the responsibility to care for each other, therefore, husband and wife should not withhold themselves sexually from one another, but should fulfil each other's needs. Although this can sometimes be challenging, the honesty I detailed earlier in this lesson (principle 6) will go a long way in helping you to understand each other's libido, and how to communicate your needs in a way that will not upset your partner. Remember, you must talk to them with love!

If you were not a virgin before you got married, remember that the type of sex you had before you got married is different from the sex you have with your spouse. If you are struggling with this aspect of your sexual intimacy with your spouse, I encourage you to get help.

How is your sexual life?

Further questions to consider?

- Are you getting sexual fulfilment? If not, have you discussed this with your spouse so you can come to the agreement on how you can get sexual fulfilment?

- Do you withhold sex from your spouse to punish them?

- Do you have difficulty communicating your sexual needs to your spouse? If yes, I encourage you to get help from an experienced and respectable couple known to both of you. Do not suffer in silence!

Conclusion:

Marriage is a wonderful lifetime commitment and union instituted by God that is sacred and must be cherished. If you want a great marriage, you should be prepared to invest your whole life into it.

The longer you have been married, the more you will find out about yourselves as individuals and as a unit.

Laying a great foundation for your marriage does not happen by accident, it requires careful planning, time and commitment.

Practical things to do:

- Plan to have bonding time together – set a day to plan all your activities for the week, so you both know what you are doing and where you are.

- Plan to get time with a couple who can help you to grow in your marriage and in your relationship with God.

- Pray together regularly.

- Go on holiday at least once or twice a year – just the two of you!!

- Read a good marriage book together and share your learning with each other.

- Model your marriage on a Bible character who inspires you to be Godly.

Lesson Two

Communication - From The Heart

What is communication?

For the purpose of this lesson, I will keep the definition of communication simple and say: it is the exchange of information between a husband and his wife. God has blessed us with the five senses (sight, hearing, taste, smell and touch).

In most cases, sight, hearing and touch are more often used together to communicate directly with others, verbally and non-verbally.

A lot has been written on this subject about listening and how couples should talk to each other.

This lesson will focus on:

- The depth that couples communicate with one another and how to improve this.
- What it takes for couples to move from shallow to deep levels of communication.
- The benefits of couples connecting their hearts to one another.

About 5 years ago, I had a knee injury due to years of pounding the pavement in training for and running the London Marathon. The injury was debilitating and restricted me from playing other sports I enjoy, like table tennis and football.

My doctor referred me to see a Physiotherapist for advice on how to manage the injury. The one I saw advise me to stop doing any contact sport for a while and take up swimming instead as the water will help to take pressure off my knee and will help my rehabilitation.

I was not excited about the thought of swimming because I could not swim, and the prospect of learning at my age was terrifying. But because I wanted to get better, I decided to go to the Crystal Palace Sports Centre, close to where I live, to register for swimming lessons, two days a week for twelve weeks.

I was glad that my wife joined on the same day to support me and to improve on her swimming skills.

The instructor took us to the shallow end first and gave us basic drills. She said that it is always good to start from the shallow end, and as one's skills gets better, one can venture into the deep end.

Week by week, I improved my skills and got better and better, and I ended up looking forward to spending more time at the deep end without any floats.

As I always look for the relevance of any new situation, I find myself relating this to marriage coaching. I thought about the depth that couples communicate with each other: whether they communicate at a shallow or deep level, how this might impact how well they know each other, and the impact each level has on the quality of their relationship. That was how this lesson came about.

Just like a swimming pool has a shallow end and deep end, couples can communicate with each other at a shallow level or at a deep level.

The shallow end of a swimming pool attracts mostly beginners and inexperienced swimmers, but as they become more competent and their confidence grows in their ability to swim, they might venture into the deep end.

Although, when swimmers become experts, they are equally relaxed swimming in the shallow and the deep end.

Through our marriage coaching for over 20 years, we find that couples who communicate at shallow levels have the following traits in common:

- They talk about mundane things: the subject matter is basic and does not require emotional vulnerability. For example, the weather, what they will have for dinner, places they can visit on holiday, who will collect the children from school, where to go for a meal or where to go shopping. They engage in chitchats because it is fun to them and they get a kick out of that. They may even talk about other people but avoid talking about themselves.

- Tiptoeing around each other: they carefully avoid discussing or dealing with difficult or sensitive subjects that will likely reveal what is going on in their hearts. So, they say what they want each other to hear. The underlying reason might be fear of reprisal on one person's part or on both of them. They would rather discuss what they want their spouse to hear and not deal with the burning issues that makes them unhappy in the marriage.

- They often struggle with insecurity: they live in fear that if their spouse knew what they are like, they may not like them. So, they behave like a Chameleon and adapt to the mood of their spouse to get by in the marriage.

On the other hand, couples who communicate at a deep level have the following traits in common:

- They openly share their thoughts, feelings and imperfections, and are received well by their spouse. They do not judge each other, are more inclined to show understanding, and are willing to help each other to overcome their weaknesses and turn them into strengths. There is a feeling of "we are in this together" about them.

- They feel secure in who they are and in their relationship with their spouse. There is no 'no go' area in their interactions with each other.

- They are happier, vulnerable, with no hidden agenda between them, they gently and firmly speak the truth with love to help each other, and they talk about meaningful things.

There are couples who are quite happy communicating at a shallow level and are quite content with that as it makes them happy. If that is how they choose to relate to one another, that is their choice and they will have to live with it. But they may be missing out on truly knowing the person they married. What their worries, fears or future aspirations are would not be known to them.

What we have found is that for couples who wish to enhance the quality of their relationship, they venture into having a deep level of communication and find this rewarding, they know their spouse better, they know what makes them tick and are aware of what could make them anxious or upset. It is the knowing of each other that is crucial here.

The more you know your spouse, the better you can relate to them. I also believe that the better connected you are to each other, the better the quality of your marriage.

What we have found in our marriage and in people who communicate at a deep level is that they feel that their hearts are connected to each other.

This feeling is one I felt when I sat Helen down one day and told her everything that happened in my life as far back as I could remember. The good, the bad and the ugly. We were probably married for 5 years then. I felt the need to share these things because I felt that we were not as close as I wanted us to be.

The more you know your spouse, the better you can relate to them.

I desired for her to be my best friend and my confidanté. Also, I did that in response to what the Bible says in **Genesis 2:25**: *'And the man and his wife were both naked and were not ashamed or embarrassed'* AMP Version.

I believe that the nakedness discussed in this passage extends beyond physical nakedness, but also to the baring of their hearts to each other.

Suffice it to say that, heart connection happens when you and your spouse communicate at a deep level.

After the chat I had with Helen, she shared what she could remember about her past with me. I believe that was the beginning of a new chapter in our marriage; when we set a new standard of openness and connectivity. I am so glad that I initiated the conversation because it resulted in both of us sharing our past with each other.

If you desire a real heart connection with your spouse, I suggest that you consider having a similar conversation with each other. Doing so might be difficult for some people, so you may need the help of a professional marriage coach to set the scene to make it easier for you to talk candidly with your spouse. Investing in a marriage coach will likely cost you some money, but let me tell you, the benefits will outweigh the amount you spend.

When I was learning how to drive, I thought it would be impossible to get the car to biting point going uphill, and I was petrified of stalling the car and allowing it to roll backwards and cause an accident. I remember talking to my instructor about this, and he assured me that at the right time, he would show me how to do it. I waited in anticipation, and when it finally came, he talked me through the procedure. I followed his instructions to the letter and I achieved the desired outcome.

I sighed with relief and glowed with excitement after I had succeeded at something I dreaded. As luck will have it, the examiner asked me to do an emergency stop as we were going uphill on the day of my test, and I did it without the car rolling back! Although the engine cut off, I managed to do the hill start, get the car to the biting point and drive off at ease.

Similarly, if you are afraid to share your past with your spouse and get the heart connection you want, a good marriage coach will talk you through what you need to do to help your situation.

When you feel that you and your spouse's hearts are connected, it will become obvious to both of you.

To get to a deep level in your relationship, I suggest that you do the exercise below.

- Have a conversation with your spouse about what you believe is hindering deep communication.

- Ask your spouse questions you've never asked before. Unpack hopes and dreams.

- Discuss what you can do together to get to know each other better and strengthen the bonds between you.

General rules for effective communication:

No matter the depth you communicate with your spouse, it is important to observe the following rules.

The Do's	The Don'ts
- **Do** pray before engaging in serious conversation. - **Do** be slow to speak and quick to listen. - **Do** give a soft answer and control your emotions. - **Do** be patient with each other. - **Do** clarify what you thought you heard before responding. For example, "so what you are saying is..."	- **Don't** allow your attention to drift. - **Don't** talk when you or your partner are physically or mentally exhausted. - **Don't** allow your expectations to consume you. - **Don't** allow the emotions of your spouse to dictate your responses. - **Don't** interrupt when one of you is speaking. - **Don't** be judgemental.

In addition to the do's and don'ts above, I would like to introduce two concepts that can help to boost better communication between you and your spouse.

These are: **Illusion of Transparency** and **Cognitive Miser.**

What is Illusion of Transparency?

The Illusion of Transparency is when someone thinks their thoughts and emotions are transparent to others when they are not, or at least not as much as they think.

Ever since I learnt this concept, I have been fascinated to understand how it affects married couples.

Assuming that your spouse knows what you are thinking or feeling without telling them may cause them to make the wrong assumption about how you are feeling. Their inability to connect with how you are feeling may cause you to feel upset, angry or unloved and this may frustrate both of you.

So, for example, your spouse looks at you and they can see you are thinking about something. They ask you what you are thinking about and you reply with, "You should know what I am thinking, how long have you known me?" and they reply with, "How do you expect me to know what you are thinking or feeling unless you tell me? If you think I am a mind reader, then know this, I am not!!"

If you have had this type of conversation in your marriage, that is the Illusion of Transparency, which causes countless issues and grief in marriages.

Why is the Illusion of Transparency an issue in a marriage?

The Illusion of Transparency is an issue in a marriage because it causes one person to have needless negative feelings towards their spouse, and if it is not dealt with sooner, they may exacerbate.

Some of our clients have expressed feelings such as: feeling unloved, frustration, hatred, irritation and second guessing each other's motives and actions.

These negative feelings can also contribute to poor conflict resolution. Thinking that your grievances are obvious to your spouse can also lead to conflict avoidance or passive aggressive behaviour. For example, thoughts like, "I shouldn't have to tell him/her why I'm upset! It should be obvious!"

Here are some suggestions to resolving the Illusion of Transparency Mindset.

Say what you're thinking. Instead of assuming that your spouse already knows what's going on in your mind, say what you are thinking! Really, it's as simple as that. Your spouse isn't a mind reader. They have their own life and their own thoughts, which preoccupy them, so it's impossible for them to notice every little detail about your life right away. Give them some grace, and if there's something you want them to pay attention to, let them know.

Shift your focus away from yourself. Do not only think of your own interest but think of the interest of your spouse. Shifting your focus away from yourself to think about your spouse's perspective will prevent you from getting stuck in your own self-perception. Learn to spend less time focused on your own thoughts and experiences, and try to see things from your spouse's view instead.

Volunteer information freely: Your spouse cannot read your mind, if you are thinking that they can, this behaviour is hurting you and your spouse, so make the decision to be open and transparent, and be the first to volunteer information about your thoughts and feelings. Doing so will be liberating for you and your spouse and will draw you closer together.

Seeing things from your spouse's perspective. This may help to reduce tension between you. See the picture below.

The picture above perfectly illustrates what goes on in a relationship when we don't see things from our spouse's perspective. Someone has to back down, be humble, and see things from your spouse's perspective.

If you decide today to see things from your spouse's point of view, do you think it will help to reduce the negative effect of Illusion of Transparency in your marriage?

If yes, how? And what will it take from you?

Further Questions to Consider:

- Can you identify instances when the Illusion of Transparency became apparent in your marriage?

- What effect did it have on you?

- What effect did it have on your spouse?

- How was this resolved, if it was ever resolved?

- Write down and discuss the benefits of giving your spouse the information they need so they don't have to guess what is going on in your mind.

I hope you have found this lesson on the Illusion of Transparency useful. I will now move on to discuss the second concept: Cognitive Miser.

So, what is Cognitive Miser?

Well, it's a term coined by Susan Fiske and Shelley Taylor, described as: the brain's tendency to seek solutions to problems that take the least mental effort. It's often said that thinking is hard, and I believe that, and because thinking is hard, most people don't want to do it, so they avoid doing it at all costs!

In Aditi's article in Psychology Today, she stated that, "We have all formed habits that enable us to virtually bypass the thinking process. We've hardwired our brains to take shortcuts. For many adults, this "non-thinking" aspect runs on autopilot as though the brain knows no other way."

In this microwave age we live in where people want instant meals without labouring to cook it, and where people can google any information they want in an instant, most people don't want to work for the information they need. As a result, most people develop a lazy mind and do not take the time to think anymore.

As a result, how couples communicate with each other is negatively impacted.

Here are a few signs that you might be a cognitive miser:

- Not fully engaging in taxing conversations that requires your input to solve a problem. If you find yourself saying to your spouse, "You are the more intellectual one, you can figure out the solution" rather than sitting down to figure out the solution together.

- When your spouse, or people you associate with, ask a question and the first thing that you say is, "I don't know."

- When you give a flippant answer to a question without thinking through what you have said. Doing this makes you seem aloof and disconnected to the subject matter.

- When you are impatient to hear the whole account of an event your spouse is trying to relay to you. You may say, "get to the point" or "I am not interested in the whole detail."

Any of the signs above may lead to poor communication between you and your spouse, which in turn, will likely cause unnecessary conflict in your marriage.

Reversing the Cognitive Miser Mindset:

Firstly, you need to admit that you have the tendency to be a cognitive miser and then make a conscious effort to train your mind to be Godly.

1 Timothy 4:7: *'Have nothing to do with godless myths and old wives' tales, rather, train yourself to be godly.'*

From the passage above, it seems that godless myths and old wives' tales are disempowering to someone who wants to live a positive and progressive life. Hence, Paul's encouragement to Timothy to train himself to be Godly – to have a God focused outlook on everything he does.

For example, God is not a God of disorder but of peace and order *(1 Corinthians 14:33)*. So, you have to make the conscious effort to be orderly, not disorderly.

Secondly, challenge your brain and mind to snap out of a lazy mindset and find new ways of doing things.

A lazy mindset may rob you and your spouse of the positive contributions you could make to improving communication between the two of you, and developing new skills.

During the first lockdown of the coronavirus pandemic in the in 2020, my wife spent a lot of time baking, which I also enjoyed. I consider myself a good cook, some people say excellent cook – so I won't take anything away from their perception of me regarding my cooking skills. However, I am useless at baking.

The reason I have been reluctant to venture into baking is because I am not used to measuring ingredients when cooking, but it is different with baking. You have to measure everything, so baking has never been attractive to me.

It occurred to me that this was a great opportunity to snap out of the cognitive miser mindset. So, I decided to challenge my brain to bake.

I got the recipe book out, and with the assistance of my wife, I managed to bake bread despite every fibre in my body resisting the need to measure the ingredients. The fun side was that our son said he had never seen us argue the way we did when my wife was trying to assist me with the baking. But I finally gave in and it was fine in the end.

I learnt something new about myself that day: when I am in an unknown territory, I become impatient, but it was a good experience for me, and I am working hard on being more patient.

It is not easy to snap out of a lazy mindset, but when you do, it is the most rewarding thing you can do for yourself and for your relationship. Plus, you may even get a bonus out of it: learning something new about yourself.

I can honestly tell you that I love baking bread now, and friends who have tasted my bread can testify how tasty my baking has become. It makes me feel good that I acquired a new skill during the lockdown.

Furthermore, my baking experience spurred me to take on the next challenge: online banking.

Since internet banking was introduced by our bank in May 1997, my wife has been on top of it, but I have not made any effort to venture into that arena. She is fascinated by technology and how it works, so she can easily adapt and follow the latest technology.

However, I am more of a laggard, but I decided to try internet banking and have become successful at it. I am elated and proud that I am conquering my lazy mindset and applying myself in areas I never did before.

I am sure I am not the only one in this boat. If you can identify with me on this matter, what are you going to do about your situation?

It is better to take action now and train your mind to respond to areas of your life and marriage you need to improve on; the positive change will be beneficial to you and your spouse.

Thirdly, overcome negative thoughts with positive ones. All the negative thoughts you tell yourself, such as, "You can't do that" should be changed to positives, and you can do this by developing a can-do attitude. Is there a project you need to embark on? Well, if so, there is no better time for you to start than now. I first thought about writing a book about 10 years ago but I kept doubting my ability to do so, and I worried about being criticised by other people. As a result, I told myself that I couldn't do it. But here I am now fighting through my demons and telling myself that I can do anything I wish through Christ, who gives me strength *(Philippians 4:13).*

I started writing at the beginning of 2020, and now I'm finishing the first draft at the end of the year. What a thrilling journey and experience. You can also talk yourself into having a can-do attitude too.

Finally, have people hold you accountable. Let your spouse and people in your circle of influence know that you have the tendency to be lazy in your thinking, and that you are working to change that.

By verbalising it to these people is victory for you because people with a lazy mindset find it difficult to verbalise what they are thinking or feeling. They are content to coast along, but you can set yourself free from what has held you down for a long time. Rejoice and be happy!

Have a can-do attitude towards work and learning new things.

Step outside your comfort zone and try new things. I remember when I admitted to being a cognitive miser, I realised that I am programmed to do things the same way all the time. For example, when I pick up a newspaper to read, the first thing I do is turn to the sports pages because that is the only section that interests me.

So, to step out of my comfort zone and develop my brain, I had to make a conscious effort to read the least interesting pages before the sports pages. This was hard for me at first, but I am glad I persevered with it due to the benefits it has given me, and how it has improved my ability to think of solutions.

Admittedly, not everyone reading this section of my book will relate to being a cognitive miser, but if you recognise yourself in what I'm saying, take action and your ability to think will improve. There are plenty of activities that encourage and train your brain to think more often, such as crosswords, sudoku or board games like Scrabble or Chess.

Conclusions:

Good communication is a lifeline to a healthy marriage, so when communication breaks down, all sorts of problems arise.

The depth couples communicate depends on how well they know each other, which also affects the quality of their relationship. Couples who communicate at a deep level seem to know each other well and feel more secure in the relationship.

It would be beneficial for couples who communicate at a shallow level to gravitate towards communicating at a deep level to enhance the quality of their marriage.

The Illusion of Transparency can cause unnecessary conflict in a marriage and affect how you and your spouse communicate with one another. To avoid this, it is advisable to give your spouse the information they need so they don't have to second guess what you are thinking or feeling.

Having a lazy mind is a sign that you are a cognitive miser, but you don't have to be that way. Make a conscious effort to develop the part of your brain that allows you to think creatively so you can enhance your wellbeing and self-esteem.

It is important to retrain your brain by taking on tasks you previously considered impossible. Doing so will enable you to reverse the cognitive miser mind-set and improve communication between you and your spouse.

Further questions to consider:

- Can a cognitive miser change their mindset?

  Absolutely! It takes determination to examine your way of thinking and admit your shortcomings.

- Discuss with your spouse how being a cognitive miser affects you.

- Is there something your spouse wants to know about you that you are holding back? Take the chance to open up or get advice from a trained marriage coach to support you, it will be beneficial to your marriage.

Lesson Three

Resolving Quarrels in Marriage

Quarrels are a natural part of married life. As marriage brings two people with different life experiences and backgrounds together under one roof, quarrels are inevitable, but they must be resolved quickly and effectively to avoid damaging the relationship.

Let us examine what the Bible says about why people quarrel.

James 4:1-2: *"What causes fights and quarrels among you? Don't they come from your desires that battles within you? You want something but don't get it. You kill and covet, but you cannot have what you want. You quarrel and fight..."*

Applying this scripture to marriage, couples generally quarrel when one of them feels that what they desire from their spouse (e.g. love, companionship, happiness, security and peace) have not been met. However, not all couples have the maturity to discuss how their desires can be met in their marriage. So, they shy away from discussing it, as it may lead to a quarrel.

Maturity has more to do with how you live your life than your age, so the maturity I refer to, is about creating a safe environment to raise any issue that makes you unhappy in your marriage.

There are different types of quarrels Helen and I have had to resolve with couples we have coached over the years. Some can be classified as trivial, and others significant.

The focus of this lesson will be on certain disagreements that may occur in your marriage, because if they are not resolved in a sensitive and timely manner, they can lead to prolonged period of unhappiness.

The Cambridge English Dictionary defines a quarrel as: "heated arguments or disagreements, typically about **trivial issues** between people who are **usually on good terms**".

You and your spouse are usually on good terms. You love each other, want to spend time with each other, care for each other and genuinely want the best for each other. However, one or both of you may sometimes allow issues to invade that bring temporary unhappiness to your marriage.

Here are some examples of issues that may cause quarrels in a marriage:

'Husband prefers to squeeze the toothpaste from the middle, but wife would prefer if they squeeze it from the bottom.'

'*Wife wants the family to move to a different neighbourhood, but the husband wants to remain where they currently live.*'

'*Husband wants to spend money on gadgets, but the wife wants them to save money for a rainy day.*'

'*Wife wants her mother to move in with them, but the husband is opposed to this idea.*'

'*Husband and wife are quarrelling about when the housework should be done. Wife wants them to clean as they go along and husband wants them done at a set time.*'

'*Wife wants the family to use Andrex toilet roll, but the husband finds it expensive and would prefer them to buy the store brand that is cheaper.*'

'*One spouse is feeling like the other is not disciplining the children enough and turning them into spoilt brats. Therefore, they want to take over the discipling of the children and set the rules for them.*'

'*The extracurricular activities the children take part in are some of the issues many couples quarrel about.*'

Because some couples could not control their temper or empathise with their spouse during a quarrel, a few couples have ended up physically or verbally abusing each other.

Admittedly, some of the examples above are significant and must be carefully thought through and discussed to reach a happy resolution. For example, the decision to have the mother in-law move in with them, the husband wanting to spend money on gadgets and the wife wanting to move neighbourhood.

These decisions have huge ramifications for the couple, so they must be carefully considered. If they cannot reach a compromise amicably, they should get the support of a professional or trusted friend that they both agree will be objective with them and impartial.

However, this chapter will focus on how couples should deal with the following types of issues: the type of toilet rolls to buy, when housework should be done, or where to squeeze the toothpaste from. These are trivial matters but some couples make a big deal of it and consequently, they quarrel continuously.

I believe all quarrels should be temporary, and should be resolved quickly, not dragged on for days, weeks, months or even years.

It is common for some couples to disagree on the same issue for years and never make the effort to resolve them. They would rather sweep them under the carpet, but by so doing, they are deferring the problems that are making them unhappy.

Later on, the issues they swept under the carpet will resurface, and in most cases, will hit them harder than before.

So, it is important to deal with problems in your marriage as and when they occur.

If you are the one who likes to drag disputes out for as long as possible rather than resolving them quickly, you need to seek help.

Why? Because it is not good for your mental health, detrimental to your spiritual wellbeing, and damaging to your marriage.

Exercise 1: Make a list of the quarrels you have had recently.

What you will probably find is that most of your rows are really trivial. If that is the case, decide to overcome them quickly. Any difficult quarrel on your list must be addressed promptly, even if it means seeking professional help.

As I said in the opening statement of this lesson, quarrels are inevitable and are part and parcel of married life. Every marriage will have its share of them, but they must be resolved with haste to avoid further damage to your marriage.

Our upbringing may be a contributory factor to how we respond and deal with quarrels.

Consider the example of Jennifer and Charles below:

Jennifer: *grew up in a home where her father abused her mother and left their lives when she was very young. So, Jennifer grew up not having a male role model, which made her feel insecure about herself, especially when around people who had a better upbringing than her. Her need for self-fulfilment is to have her emotional needs met.*

So, the three things she would appreciate from Charles are for him to:

- Be emotionally connected.
- Spend time with her.
- Affirm and assure her.

Charles: *had a difficult relationship with his father and was expected to be a high-flyer. He grew up and became independent, self-assured and a self-starter, but devoid of showing his emotions. He considers showing his emotions a sign of weakness, but deep down, he enjoys praise from people to feel fulfilled.*

So, the three things he would appreciate from Jennifer are for her to:

- Be positive all the time.
- Recognise and acknowledge the good things he is doing.
- See the good in him and don't point out the bad.

Exercise 2: Identify the reasons why Charles and Jennifer may quarrel in their marriage.

When you have done this, discuss your upbringing with your spouse and see whether it has any relevance to the disagreements you are having.

When you have this discussion, it is important to set ground rules to make it constructive and beneficial to both of you.

A great Bible passage that can help with this is: **James 1:19** *'My dear brothers and sisters, take note of this: Everyone should be quick to listen, slow to speak and slow to become angry...'*

An example of what quick to listen and slow to speak looks like:

- Training ourselves to listen to the whole story before diving in with our opinions.

- Controlling the words, we use.

- Not blurting out anything that comes into our heads.

Furthermore, to benefit from this exercise, you have to be totally honest with yourself and with each other. You might be surprised with your findings.

Marriage is a union between two individuals who bring their own life experiences, formed from their family or the environment they grew up. For the most part, your life experiences are different from your spouse's.

As a result, the differences may cause you to see and perceive issues that comes up in your marriage differently. We get great benefits from our differences, which enhance the quality of our marriage. However, we equally bring some negative traits into our marriage that can have a detrimental effect.

Exercise 3: Write out a profile of yourselves, your background, how your parents or significant adults in your family or community dealt with quarrels.

Are there similarities in how they dealt with disagreements and how you are dealing with them in your marriage?

If there are similarities, write them down and discuss how they play out in your marriage.

This exercise should help you to understand each other a little bit better.

Helen and I quarrel, but it is rare these days because we understand each other's trigger points, which we learnt by working hard to support each other and help each other to control them. Praise God that we have moved away from how things were in the early days of our marriage when we did not have the word of God to guide us.

Back then, rowing was a big part of our marriage because I wanted things done my way, but if I did not get my way, I would argue with Helen and expect her to back down.

But now when we quarrel, it is an indication that one of us or both of us are not paying attention to our needs. So, we stop and talk about what is really going on in our hearts.

The analogy that helps us with this is: imagine driving your car over a bump and you hear an unusual noise you have never heard before. The natural thing to do is to stop your car as soon as possible to check what that noise was about.

So, for us, the unusual noise from the car is when we dispute. It is a sign for us to stop and check what has gone wrong with our relationship, and most importantly, what we are learning from that experience.

What are you learning from your quarrels?

My wife and I often tell couples that the goal is not to win the argument, it is about what they can *learn about themselves.*

Often times when couples argue, they are concerned about protecting their own side of the argument and will do anything to prove that their partner is in the wrong.

But shifting the focus onto what they are learning about themselves puts the focus on them rather than their spouse. Couples who make this a habit will learn something new about themselves. This should help them to be more aware of the potential issues that could lead them to quarrel, so they can address them quickly.

These are some of the things our clients have said they learnt about themselves when they looked into this question:

"I realised that I am a selfish person, and that is borne out of my competitive nature, always wanting to win at all costs. With me, even board games are not fun unless I win. I had the same attitude in my marriage until I took the time to examine what I am learning about myself when we quarrel. Now, I don't compete with my wife anymore, which has made me more relaxed around her. I no longer see her as a challenger, I now see her as a teammate with the same goal to win together."

"I was raised to believe that I should not be a doormat for any man to walk on. So, I wanted to prove to my husband that I was not someone he could push around. But when I examined what I am learning about myself when we quarrel, it helped me to understand that holding onto my pride is not good for our relationship. So, I decided to let go of it, and doing so has led us to having meaningful discussions, listening and reasoning with one another. As a result, there is so much peace in the house"

From the examples above, when couples can identify what they are learning about themselves, and if they make every effort to change them, their tolerance level will increase, which will help them to be emotionally mature enough to deal with subsequent quarrels.

I am aware that not everyone will appreciate the idea of examining what they are learning about themselves when they argue with their spouse. There are some people who will not take kindly to this way of thinking but will want to win the argument.

If winning the argument is your goal, you are looking for ways to feed your pride and ego – which is probably the cause of the quarrel in the first place.

It is important for couples to know that their attitude to rows in their marriage will reveal a lot about their character, and those willing to consider what they are learning about themselves go on to have happy marriages. Sadly, those who do not, will likely remain unhappy because they have not addressed this issue.

<u>Steps to resolving quarrels in marriage</u>

There are two important qualities of a Godly person (someone who has committed themselves to loving God and obeying his commands) that I've found useful in my work as a marriage coach. They are **Humility** and **Obedience** to the scriptures.

For me, these qualities are inseparable, and any couple who understands and lives by them will have less quarrels and will ultimately be happier in their marriage.

Humility is defined as "the state or quality of being humble; a recognition of self in relation to God". I think it is important to understand how humility works – humility towards God first will help us to understand how to be humble toward each other.

Check out this scripture that sums it up succinctly: **James 4:10** *"Humble yourselves before the Lord, and he will lift you up"*.

Humility towards each other becomes easier to manage when the two of you make humility to God a priority in your marriage.

Then, it might help you to understand and implement the next passage of scripture:

Ephesians 4:2: *"Be completely humble and gentle, be patient, bearing with one another in love."*

For me, humility is one of the greatest virtues to quell quarrels. I love the way Paul addressed this subject with the church in Ephesus; if couples could follow the order, he arranged the virtues listed in the above passage, I believe they will lessen the quarrels they have.

Humility will lead them to being gentle, being patient and bearing with one another in love. Therefore, they can handle disagreements in their marriage and bring glory to God by their obedience to the scriptures.

Take the example of Mr & Mrs B during one of our coaching sessions. They were arguing intensely with each other, so I asked them to make a list of what they quarrel about.

See their list below:

- Not putting the car key in the right place.
- Leaving cupboard open in the kitchen.
- Not emptying the dishes rack but adding more dishes.
- Bed not made in the morning.

During the course of the session, we discussed how they feel being humble towards each other would help to quell their quarrels. They looked at each other and said, "that seems to be the problem". So, I encouraged them to memorise a passage of scripture about humility and commit to putting it into practise.

They did, and at the next session, they reported that humility towards each other had helped them to quarrel less. They also put the following into practice:

- Do bring up issues in a non-accusatory manner – give your spouse the benefit of the doubt.
- Do listen to your spouse. If your spouse says that your behaviour upsets them, make every effort to stop that behaviour pattern. If you do not, it might lead to resentment towards you. Be quick to listen and slow to speak, and even slower to become angry.
- Do agree to resolve issues by coming to a compromise.
- Do not hold grudges or harbour bitterness, but bring issues up quickly so your heart will not be hardened towards your spouse.

- Do not deliberately hurt your spouse. I know couples who do this to each other just for a laugh, but it always ends up with one person's feelings being hurt.

Psalm 25:9 tells us that *"He (God) guides the humble in what is right and teaches them his way."*

Allow the word of God to guide and teach you. If you do, you will see the benefits to you and your spouse. So, do this on a regular basis and pray together, specifically about your marriage.

Further questions to consider:

- Are you willing to be humble towards each other?
- If not, why not? Consider the benefits of being humble towards each other and think about what it will bring to your marriage.
- Discuss and pray together for God to help you keep the decisions you make to be humble towards each other.

Obedience: the biblical definition means 'to hear, trust, submit and surrender to God and His word'. In other words, whenever we read the word of God and it challenges our behaviour or thought, we have to let it go and adopt what the Bible says. There are no ifs or buts.

Through counselling couples, the reason so many Church-goers struggle in their marriage is because they have ifs and buts and make excuses not to obey biblical instructions. Instead, they rationalise the scriptures.

For example, take **Matthew 6:12:** *"Forgive us the wrongs we have done, as we forgive the wrongs that others have done to us."* (GNB version)

Jesus taught that his followers should ask for forgiveness for the wrongs they have done, and in turn, they should forgive those who have wronged them.

This seems simple enough for anyone who says they believe in the Bible. But for some inexplicable reason, some 'believers' have told us that they find it difficult to forgive their spouse of the wrongs they had done to them.

Through counselling couples, the reason so many Church-goers struggle in their marriage is because they have ifs and buts and make excuses not to obey biblical instructions. Instead, they rationalise the scriptures.

Also, we have known couples who go to church and read their Bible say that they have forgiven their spouse of the wrongs they had done to them, and yet they continue to bring the same issue up whenever they quarrel.

The two examples above do not show **obedience** to the scriptures on their part. We see old wounds arise too often and it makes us question the foundation of their faith and their understanding of the word of God.

An important question for believers of the Bible to consider:

In what ways have you rationalised the word of God as an individual or as a couple and made excuses for not obeying them?

The behaviour I have noticed in some people who read the Bible and don't put it into practice, is similar to my behaviour before I studied it.

When Helen and I were a young married couple, and before I came to know Christ, I blamed her for everything that went wrong in our marriage to the point that I resented her in my heart and had an attitude towards her. I hardly took responsibility for anything, because to me, it will be a sign of weakness. However, I knew deep down that I was in the wrong, but admitting it was difficult. Looking back to those days, I can see how selfish, arrogant, prideful and insecure I had become.

I am grateful to God for giving me the opportunity to study the Bible, and for the first time, I realised the damaging effect my selfishness, arrogance, pride and insecurities caused to our marriage. As a result, I made a decision to repent – make a commitment to God and to Helen that I will change my ways and be obedient to the word of God. I am grateful to God that I am true to the commitment I made on 24 April 1989 because it has helped to minimise the number of quarrels between Helen and I.

Do we have disagreements? Of course, we do. It would not be a good relationship if we did not disagree on some things, but we have both realised that obedience to the word of God helps us to stem quarrels and to resolve issues quickly.

Having someone explain the teachings in the Bible to me helped to expose my character flaws (selfishness, arrogance, pride and insecurities), and it also gave me the insight that I could overcome them. Now I am aware of them, I fight against them, refusing to allow them into my life. I don't always succeed, but when I falter, I do my best to apologise to my wife and get back on track.

I now consciously solicit input from my wife, children and friends who have my best interests at heart, on what they think I need to change about myself for me to be the best I can be.

This has benefitted me immensely, so you may want to go through the same exercise to see what people will reveal about your character.

In their book, Boundaries in Marriage, Dr Cloud and Dr Townsend made this point beautifully – "We all have aspects of our personalities and character that we do not know about". As King David said in **Psalm 19:12** *'who can discern his errors? Forgive my hidden faults'*

You see, David knew there were things about himself that he did not know. Similarly, your spouse, children and friends, who really care about you, may know things about you that you may not know.

Asking them to tell you what they believe you need to change, and committing to change them, will be beneficial to you as a person, to your marriage and will improve the relationship with everyone who cares about you.

I am aware that soliciting feedback is easy for some people and difficult for others. Please see suggested example on how to go about this below:

"I am working on changing some things about me that I believe will make our relationship better, and I believe you can help me since you are the person who knows me better than anyone else."

"Your input is vital to me. Please could you kindly tell me the things you see in me that I could change to make our relationship better? If you cannot think of anything right now, that is fine, but please take the time to think and let me know when you have some suggestions."

I vividly remember asking Helen for her input to help me change, and she gave me the following ideas: At the time, I was financially indiscipline and this was putting the family finances in debt.

- Helping out with housework, cooking, cleaning, ironing and getting the children ready for school.

- Ensuring that there is fuel in the car and not leaving it for her to do all the time.

I humbly accepted them without complaining or challenging the things she said because I needed to change. I am grateful to her to this day.

When I suggest this approach to couples as a marriage coach, some of them sneer at it, others reject it and for those who have adopted this approach, have noticed that they quarrel less.

Follow-up calls to couples who rejected this approach revealed that they continue to quarrel, and sadly, some have even walked away from the relationship.

Further questions to consider:

- Are you willing to seek input from your spouse and the people in your sphere of influence on the things you need to change to improve your relationships?

- If the answer is no, why is that?

I would encourage you to honestly answer this question and to also seek professional help if you need to. If you don't answer this question in the affirmative, you and your spouse will not be able to minimise the quarrels in your marriage, and both of you will continue to be unhappy in the relationship. Is that what you really want?

I suspect not. So, I would implore you to do the honourable thing and seek help.

Conclusion:

Quarrels are part and parcel of marriage, but they must be resolved quickly. When you disagree, do not think of winning the argument, instead, think of what you could learn about yourself. This attitude will help you to modify your behaviour and assist you to meet each other's desire for love, companionship, happiness, security and peace.

For couples who are believers in the message of the Bible, humility and obedience are excellent virtues to hold on to as they will equip you with the tools you need to deal with issues that could potentially lead to damaging rows. Failure to adhere to putting the scriptures into practise is hypocrisy and unhelpful to you and to your marriage.

Lesson
Four

Dealing With Hurts

This chapter will discuss what hurtful acts are and how to deal with them in your marriage.

Definition of hurtful acts:

In the context of marriage, hurtful acts are things a spouse says or does to their partner that causes emotional, physical or psychological pain. For the most part, the pain occurs when the person on the receiving end of the hurtful acts feels disrespected, undervalued and betrayed.

Disrespect: Has an undertone of rudeness and taking your spouse for granted instead of affording them the respect they deserve as your life partner. Not saying thank you to your spouse when they have done something for you. Another example includes humiliating them in the presence of other people for something you consider they have not done to your expectation.

Undervalued: People feel undervalued when they don't feel appreciated, acknowledged or recognised. In the context of marriage, people may feel undervalued when their contribution of money, time and commitment to grow the marriage has not been recognised. No matter how hard they try, they don't have equal say in the relationship and are expected to play second fiddle to their spouse.

Betrayed: Betrayal means an act of deliberate disloyalty; like when you tell other people your spouse's secret, something they have told you in confidence and expect you not to share it with anyone else. Other examples include having an affair, reneging on an agreed plan, and being deceitful.

EXERCISE ONE:

Think about a time that you have disrespected, undervalued or betrayed your spouse. Or better still, when your spouse told you they felt disrespected, undervalued or betrayed. How was this resolved?

If it were never resolved, I would encourage you and your spouse to discuss the incident and reach a resolution. If you are not able to manage this by yourselves, it's always a good idea to get help to resolve it. If you don't, the issue may create a barrier between you and could prevent you from being as close as you would like to be.

In my experience from working with couples, hurtful acts are more painful because they are things the victim did not anticipate when they went into the relationship.

Couples hurt each other either **intentionally** or **unintentionally**.

Intentional hurt is a deliberate act to upset your spouse. For example, something your spouse has told you they don't like, or upsets them, and you know it, but you keep doing it.

In one of the workshops my wife and I ran on this subject, these are the things that couples shared about how they intentionally hurt their spouse. Please fasten your seat belts to read them because some might amaze and shock you.

1. Left bills unpaid.

2. Speaking rudely to spouse by saying unkind things.

3. Deliberately withholding sex from him.

4. Purposefully had an affair to hurt my spouse.

5. Keeping malice and holding grudges.

6. Unkempt – deliberately not looking after myself.

7. Going to bed late and at times sleeping on the sofa.

8. Taking advantage of my spouse's good nature.

9. Not paying much attention to my spouse by neglecting their needs.

10. Deliberately going over agreed budget to hurt him.

11. Not showing the full respect my spouse deserves.

12. Ignoring her when she is saying something to me.

13. Ignoring text messages and not replying on time.

14. Threatening my spouse with divorce.

If you or your spouse cannot identify with any of the behaviours listed above, perhaps you can compile your own list of how you intentionally hurt each other.

I find that when I write things down, it helps me to focus and assists me when I am discussing issues with my wife.

One thing is guaranteed, you know for sure how you intentionally hurt your spouse. By writing it down, hopefully it will help you to connect with your heart and realise how your behaviour is affecting them.

Also, be aware that any iota of insincerity on your part in honestly identifying how you intentionally hurt your spouse may pull you apart instead of drawing you closer to one another.

How will you know if you are being insincere in doing this self-assessment exercise?

I think the answer is when you justify or minimise your behaviour and consider them as unimportant.

If you are a Christian, you know that God knows the thoughts in your heart and knows the things you do to intentionally hurt your spouse. If anything, this should motivate you to be open and honest when you do this exercise. *Psalm 44:21: would not God have discovered it, since he knows the secrets of the heart?*

If you are open and honest with your answers to this exercise, you are on the trajectory to improving relationship with your spouse.

Conversely, if you are dishonest with your answers, you are missing a great opportunity to correct the mistakes you have been making in your relationship with your spouse, and the issues that are causing you pain will remain. The choice is yours.

Remember, **Galatians 6:7** '...*God cannot be mocked; a man reaps what he sows*'

Until you fully understand how your spouse feels about how you intentionally hurt them, you will not be able to make a lasting change. Any change you make will be temporary.

I would strongly advise that you get rid of whatever you are intentionally doing to hurt your spouse.

Unintentional Hurts: These are things couples do accidentally that hurts their spouse.

A great passage of scripture that highlights this notion is *Leviticus 5:17: "If anyone sins and does what is forbidden in any of the Lord's commands, even though they do not know it, they are guilty and will be held responsible."*

The above scripture shows that couples should examine how they unintentionally hurt each other even though they might not know it, but when their spouse brings it up, they should take responsibility for the issues that have been raised. Then take action to address them so they no longer become an issue.

Again, in one of the seminars Helen and I ran on this subject, these are some of the things participants said their spouse told them they unintentionally did that hurt them.

Now they are aware of those things, they have made a conscious effort not to do them again.

1. Leaving dirty washing around the house.

2. Dishing out food for himself first before guests.

3. We work for ourselves and employ staff – my spouse said I do not give her a voice and I am disrespectful to her at business meetings. Also, I show more respect to colleagues than I do to her.

4. Talk down about her family.

5. Continuously using phrases/words my wife does not like, this intensifies any argument.

6. Talking with my mouth full of food.

7. Not taking care of the children to remove some of the pressure.

8. Not replacing the toilet rolls when it is finished / or putting it the wrong way around.

9. Shower head put right at the top, forgets to bring it down to my level. I am the smallest person in the house, and I have to keep stretching to bring the shower head down most days.

10. Pulling the duvet off at night and I feel the chill, especially during the winter months.

I would encourage you and your spouse to create time to talk about how you unintentionally hurt each other before they become big issues and lead to resentment.

Comparing the two lists, it is surprising that from the seminar we ran, couples do more things to intentionally hurt each other than unintentionally.

Further studies need to be done to ascertain whether this is a common pattern of behaviour among couples generally. Perhaps you and your spouse may want to do the same exercise and discover how this pattern of behaviour plays out in your marriage. You never know what you will find.

Now we have discussed how couples hurt each other intentionally and unintentionally, I would like to move on to talk about the possible root cause.

How do we learn this pattern of behaviour?

Our life experiences are different, and these affect how we feel, think and express ourselves. For some of us, shouting, fighting, deceit, fits of rage and infidelity are common in our families, so we carry them into our marriage.

For some people, the pattern of behaviour they brought into their marriage is acceptable and they don't complain about it, so they carry on since they do not know any better.

But for others, when they compare the pattern of behaviour to the Bible, they are alarmed and would like to adopt the standards of what is written inside. Some adopt the standards of the Bible quicker than others, and still, some people do not accept it at all and would choose to follow the pattern they have always known, which involves living a life full of lies, deceit, selfishness and hatred towards other people.

I am one of those who grew up in an environment where lies, fits of rage, deceit, infidelity and shouting was part of my life, and I carried this into my marriage, until I came to know Christ and his teaching, then things changed for me and my wife. You will see examples of this further on in this chapter and in other parts of this book.

For the purpose of the next exercise, I will call those living according to Colossians 3:8-9 — living by the standards of the 'world,' and those who are living according to Colossians 3:12-14, will call — living by the standards of God.

So, we see two possible standards that are before people today, whether they want to follow the standard of the 'world' or the standard of God as laid out in the Bible.

The standards of the 'world' have consequences, but the standards of God, found in the Bible, have blessings.

God has given all people the freedom of choice, so no one should make someone else do what they don't want to do. It is up to individuals to make their own choices. Similarly, everyone must decide which standard they wish to uphold in their marriage.

Joshua 24:15: *"But if serving the Lord is undesirable to you, then choose for yourselves this day whom you will serve, whether the gods your forefathers served beyond the River, or the gods of the Amorites in whose land you are living. But as for me and my household, we will serve the Lord."*

Joshua was calling the people of Israel to a decision to choose which God they will serve. He also made it clear to them that he and his household will serve the Lord.

I encourage you and your spouse to choose to follow the standards of God.

Examples of standards of the 'world':

Colossians 3:8-9: *"... you must also rid yourselves of all such things as these: anger, rage, malice, slander, and filthy language from your lips. 9 Do not lie to each other..."*

Not only do the standards of the world cause pain in marriages, they also have a detrimental effect on people's health and general wellbeing.

Please see the table below:

	Definition	Effect on health or emotions
Anger	An emotion characterised by hatred towards someone or something you feel has deliberately done you wrong.	Can be harmful to your body in the long term. Prolonged stress hormones that accompany anger can destroy neurons in areas of the brain associated with judgement and short-term memory, which can also weaken the immune system.
Rage	Often used to denote hostile aggression towards someone who has wronged us.	If left unchecked, rage can lead to depression and anxiety.

Malice	The desire to inflict injury, harm or suffering on another person out of deep-seated meanness. Also, it is a form of silent treatment towards another person.	This type of behaviour affects someone's emotions first and foremost because the silent treatment is one of the worst behaviours couples or lovers can exhibit to each other. For a relationship to work, there must be a willingness to communicate desires and
		feelings towards one another. Where there is malice, the opportunity to express these feelings is removed. It is even worse if the two people live together, as the sight of each other will most certainly engender negative feelings, which are not conducive to health and wellbeing.
Slander	Making a false spoken statement to damage a person's reputation.	Once someone's reputation has been damaged, it affects their mental health, mood and wellbeing. It takes a while to redress the damage done, and sometimes, it is irretrievable, so the victim must live with the damaged reputation for the rest of their lives. What a way to treat someone you profess to "love".

Filthy language	An offensive word or phrase used as an expression of anger. For example, a swear word; dirty talk, cursing or foul language.	What goes on in someone's mind when they use filthy language in conversation with their spouse beats me. It has health and emotional implications for both of them. For the perpetrator, the health implications are similar to anger, and it has
		the propensity to trigger the negative hormones in the body that could lead to a heart attack if not checked. And for the victim, filthy language is a form of abuse and could lead them to depression, insecurity, fear, disappointment and a sad state of mind, which will be injurious to their health and emotional wellbeing.
Lying	To say or write something you know is not true. Why would someone do this to the person they "love?"	Lying doesn't necessarily cause health implications, but it does trigger emotional trauma. Lying undermines trust and it is tantamount to wickedness from the liar to the victim. It baffles me that someone in love with another person would lie to them.

Some of the people I know whose lives are characterised by the standard of the 'world' are usually unhappy with their life and they want other people around them to be unhappy too, which is a sad situation to be in.

However, there is hope for those who wish to adopt the standards of God and the benefits it brings to people's life.

Colossians 3:12-14 *"...as God's chosen people, holy and dearly loved, clothe yourselves with compassion, kindness, humility, gentleness and patience. 13 Bear with each other and forgive one another if any of you has a grievance against someone. Forgive as the Lord forgave you. 14 And over all these virtues put on love, which binds them all together in perfect unity."*

To be clothed with the qualities Paul listed in his writing to the church in Colossae means that these qualities must be visible to you and all those associated with you. When a man wears a beautiful tie or a woman a beautiful dress, it is noticeable to onlookers. Similarly, these qualities should be noticeable about you to your spouse and your associates.

Let us examine these qualities in a bit more detail.

Compassion: According to Merriam-Webster Dictionary, compassion is the "sympathetic consciousness of others' distress together with the desire to alleviate it". Applying this definition to dealing with hurts in marriage will be like you recognising how much distress your hurtful behaviour causes, and to stop that pattern of behaviour. It is not just about feeling sorry for your actions, it is about you taking action to stop hurting your spouse.

Kindness: The Oxford Dictionary definition: "the state of treating people with respect, favour and affection". These can be expressed in words or actions.

Consider what the relationship with your spouse will look like if both of you decide to always be kind to each other. I pray that this will motivate you to change your behaviour.

Gentleness: The Oxford Dictionary definition states that gentleness is: "the quality of being calm". Just being around people with this quality is inspiring; nothing phases them and they appear to be in control of their emotions. Imagine you and your spouse treating each other this way, how much less pain you will cause each other.

Patience: The Oxford Dictionary defines patience as "the ability to accept a delay or something annoying without complaining". Whoa! I must admit, this is a hard one to take. However, couples who put this quality into practise in their marriage will be able to bear with one another, in love.

Of all the qualities Paul mentioned in the scripture above, humility stands out as the quality that holds everything together. Humility is accepting that we are imperfect and willing to be corrected. Also, a humble person will be the first to say sorry when they know that they are wrong.

Alongside humility, another quality we have found useful in our work with couples in dealing with hurts in marriage is the idea of Radical Forgiveness.

Radical forgiveness is surrendering the right to retaliate against someone who hurts you.

So, what is Radical Forgiveness?

Radical Forgiveness is surrendering the right to retaliate against someone who hurts you.

To radically forgive someone who has hurt you is not easy, but not impossible. What we have found in our work with couples is that when the offender shows understanding of how their words or actions have hurt their spouse; acknowledges that they have hurt them; and displays sincere remorse about what they have done, and pledged not to do so again, it makes it easier to forgive.

In most cases, the offended person just wants the offender to acknowledge that they have done wrong and feel that they are willing to make a lasting change not to repeat the same offence.

For example:

Sanji and Sonya: Just before they got married, Sonya asked Sanji about his finances as a single man and whether he had any debt. She was of course a very financially disciplined person, who hates being in debt. He lied to her that he did not have any debts because he was afraid that if he declared them, she may pull out of the relationship, because he owed about £5k in credit card debt, and of course, paying interests.

About six months into their marriage, the amount of debt he owed came to light. She expressed her disappointment and asked why he had lied to her before they got married, when she specifically asked to know whether he had debts.

Sonya was hurt by this and told him that she will find it difficult to trust him ever again, because if he lied to her about his debts so he could marry her, what else has he lied about?

He explained that he was afraid that she might decide against marrying him if he had declared his debts and asked for forgiveness.

What Sanji did not realise was that trust was a big issue for Sonya. She had seen how her older sister's husband had lied about his finances, about his job and how that destroyed their marriage. Her sister ended up suffering a mental breakdown that required hospitalisation.

So, she said that they will need help to overcome his lies and suggested that they go and see a marriage counsellor.

She wanted some boundaries around their marriage and did not want the pattern of lies to continue in their relationship.

During the counselling sessions, the idea of Radical Forgiveness was presented to her. She wanted to do so, but of course; it was difficult.

The counsellor asked him what he could do to reassure his wife that (a) he won't lie to her again, and (b) he will not accumulate any more debts because of his indiscipline with money. He realised that until he made that commitment and became a man of his word, it would be hard for his wife to practice Radical Forgiveness.

He agreed to the following plans:

- Cut up the credit cards.
- Have a plan to repay his debts within agreed timeframe.
- Stick to an agreed budget he will not go over.
- Try and get a higher paid job to earn more money.
- Discuss any expenditure he wants to make with his wife.
- Agreed that his wife should oversee their financial affairs since she was better at managing money than him.

He worked hard at keeping to the agreed plans, and within 2 months, he got a higher paid job, so he was able to pay off his debts within a year.

However, when the offender is in denial of what they have done wrong and gaslight the victim, it makes it difficult to forgive.

Radical forgiveness becomes easier when the offender acknowledges the wrongs they have done to hurt their spouse; are remorseful about their actions, and are serious about making amends. We are all fallible and can fail our spouse at one time or another, intentionally or unintentionally.

The offender must consistently prove that they will keep their side of the bargain to be transparent in addressing what they had done wrong to hurt their spouse. Any slip up will create doubt in the victim's mind.

It will take time for the offended to forgive completely, but they will eventually get there when the offender proves that they have changed their ways.

Take a look at our second couple below:

Mr and Mrs Willis have been married for 10 years and have two children. Mr Willis was away from home on business trips, usually for about two weeks at a time. His wife had an affair with his friend, who lives close to them, while he was away.

After a few years, Mrs Willis felt guilty and wanted to end the relationship with his friend as she still loved her husband and didn't want to lose him. Her lover was not happy with this and decided to hurt both Mr and Mrs Willis. So, he decided to call Mr Willis and tell him about the affair with his wife.

Mr Willis was so distraught by this news, and he and his wife agreed to get help.

I vividly remember him sobbing uncontrollably during the first session as he asked his wife why she had an affair. This question preoccupied his mind throughout the session as he kept repeating it several times.

His wife was equally distraught and kept apologising and pleading for forgiveness.

We listened to both of them and told them that as Christian marriage coaches, the one thing we know and would recommend to them is to believe that God can help them to heal and restore the loving relationship they once had.

We advised that they needed to take proactive action to rebuild their marriage.

We shared **Matthew 7:24-25:** *"Therefore everyone who hears these words of mine and puts them into practice is like a man who built his house on the rock. The rain came down, the streams rose and the winds blew and beat against that house; yet it did not fall, because it had its foundation on the rock."* The rock stands for the word of God.

Mr and Mrs Willis agreed to put the word of God into practice in their life and marriage.

After a few sessions, Mrs Willis reassured her husband that it was a mistake that should never have happened. His absence from home made her feel lonely, and when he returned home, he only focused on their two children, so she felt neglected.

As we explored the reasons his wife gave for having the affair, she realised that they were not tenable.

The more he listened to her, the more hurt he felt, so there was no way he could overcome the hurt.

As we introduced the word of God at each session, Mr Willis' trust in God grew and he was able to radically forgive his wife. He agreed to try and rebuild their marriage again.

So, what action did they take?

- Regular holidays so they could spend more time together.
- Mr Willis quit his job and found one nearer to home.

- They became more actively involved in their church community.

As a result of them reasoning with each other and deciding to take steps to rebuild their marriage, they are living happily together, enjoying each other's company and growing in their knowledge of the word of God.

However, when couples refuse to practise radical forgiveness, the offended holds the offender as a prisoner, which causes the offender to live in fear. Consequently, the love between them may slowly die and they may both remain in a loveless marriage.

Take the example of another couple, **_Mr and Mrs Yanis_**. By coincidence, Mr Yanis went through his wife's mobile phone and saw text messages and pictures from another man. The contents proved that she was having an affair.

He confronted his wife with the evidence and she admitted to having an affair because she felt neglected and unloved by her husband.

Although she knew her reasons were inexplicable, she wanted her husband to try and understand and was willing to end the affair immediately.

However, Mr Yanis did not understand why his wife felt neglected and unloved, but he worked seven days a week to provide for his family, so he wasn't able to spend much time with them.

After a series of counselling sessions, they both realised that they needed to work on their marriage. She pleaded for forgiveness and he said he had forgiven her. They worked through their struggles and things appeared to be going well for them.

However, whenever they had a disagreement, he would always remind her of the affair and threaten to tell their children or divorce her, which is an example of what happens when the offended refuses to practise radical forgiveness.

Suffice is to say that any married person having an affair betrays the vows they made on their wedding day before God and everyone present. This is as grievous a sin, an act of betrayal one can commit against their spouse.

When people don't practice radical forgiveness, like Mr Yanis, the wound is re-opened during quarrels, which causes unhappiness and resentment.

Mr and Mrs Yanis are still together but in a toxic and loveless marriage. Prayerfully, one day he will realise that his lack of forgiveness is not good for him or their marriage.

With our God, there is always hope.

If you and your spouse are struggling with the pain you have caused each other, either intentionally or unintentionally, I encourage you to set yourselves on the path of radical forgiveness and trust God to meet you on that path.

If you do, things will work out well for both of you, like it did for Mr and Mrs Willis and Sanji and Sonya. **With our God, there is always hope.**

Here are a few practical suggestions on how you can deal with pain in your marriage:

Firstly, learn to listen and understand why your spouse is hurting. Put yourself in their shoes to feel their pain.

Empathy is difficult for most people, because in the heat of a disagreement, most people are preoccupied with getting their own point across rather than listening. As a result, they miss the crucial point their spouse is making about what is hurting them.

As I wrote this section, I had a conversation with a friend who said he was in a bad state. He and his wife were not seeing eye-to-eye because of what he had said to his family about her. As a result, his family are at odds with her, and he has been pleading for her to make peace with them, but to no avail.

After listening to his lament, I advised him to take time out and write how he thinks his wife felt about the situation.

When he thinks he understands how his wife feels about the incident and feels remorseful, he should then approach her in humility and share his understanding, listen to what she has to say, and be ready to accept whatever she says. I also advised him to apologise with all sincerity for his irresponsible behaviour.

The offender must be true to their word and not repeat the same mistake again, which will then help the victim to heal quickly.

From my experience working with couples in conflict, when the victim senses that the offender fully understands their feelings and how they have hurt them, it becomes easier to forgive and move on.

The offender must be true to their word and not repeat the same mistake again, which will then help the victim to heal quickly.

How good are you at listening to your spouse when they are trying to talk to you about how you are hurting them?

How good are you at admitting that you are in the wrong and are ready to modify your behaviour?

Consider the example of Zacchaeus in *Luke 19:1-10*. He was willing to instantly address the wrong he had done - taking more money from people than he should have, in his role as a tax collector. When Jesus noticed him on the Sycamore Fig Tree and asked to stay at his house, Zacchaeus realised the error of his ways and was willing to make amends immediately. Usually, people with this attitude see the error of their ways and are ready to modify their behaviour instantly and apologise to the people they have offended.

How good are you at apologising when you have done something to hurt your spouse?

Your answers to these questions will determine how quickly you right the wrongs you have made to hurt your spouse.

In addition to listening with intent to understand and modify your behaviour, the second thing we noticed that helped couples in our care is to replace bad habits with good ones.

Most things couples do or say to hurt their spouse can be classified as bad habits, and we all have bad habits that irritates our spouse no matter how Godly we are. While writing this chapter, I wanted to find out what my bad habits were, so I asked my wife. These are the things she said:

- Flatulence in the bedroom at night.
- Putting the toilet roll the wrong way around.
- Telling the same jokes over and over again!

I also asked our son who still lives at home, and he said I should get to the point when talking to him instead of giving a lecture. If you have adult children living with you, does that sound familiar? If yes, I encourage you to do the same exercise.

My initial reaction was to justify myself and prove them wrong, but then I thought about it and decided to take what they said onboard and commit to changing these bad habits, which has improved our relationship.

If you are not prepared to ask your spouse and children (if they live with you) about your bad habits, they will continue to be issues in your marriage and prevent you from having a great relationship with your family.

I know you are reading this book because you want to have a healthy marriage, so if you take the plunge, swallow your pride and ask your spouse and children what your bad habits are, make every effort to change them.

If you believe in the Bible, I suggest that you look for relevant Bible scriptures that will help you, etch them onto your heart, pray regularly about them, and ask God to give you the strength to overcome them.

For me, the following passages are helping me to overcome my bad habits.

Hebrews 12:1: *"Therefore, since we are surrounded by such a great cloud of witnesses, let us throw off everything that hinders and the sin that so easily entangles..."*

The scripture above is useful to me because it makes me look at what may be hindering my relationship with my family and make every effort to resolve to change them.

Proverbs 11:14: *"For lack of guidance a nation falls, but victory is won through many advisers."*

I can honestly say that I am reaping the benefits of allowing my family to advise me by pointing out things I need to change.

In addition to praying about them, occasionally ask your family whether you are making progress in the decisions you have made to listen and replace bad habits with good ones.

After committing to get rid of bad habits, the third step I recommend is for you and your spouse to agree to having an iron-sharpening iron relationship.

Proverbs 27:17: *"As iron sharpens iron, so one person sharpens another."*

I remember going into a butcher's shop one day and asking how often they sharpen their knives to ensure that the piece of meat is cut fine, and they told me they do it regularly. I asked him to put a figure to the number of times, and he said perhaps about 100 times a day, sometimes even more depending on how busy they are.

Applying this concept to marriage: two individuals are brought together, and as they live with one another and interact with each other, they see things in each other that can be improved. So, they are expected to give and receive input from each other to improve their life. For those who believe in the Bible, not only do they help each other to be the best they can for each other, they are expected to help each other to be the best they can be for God.

Take the example of Joshua and Hana:

Joshua and Hana agreed to give each other the licence to bring up any issues they see in each other that could be improved. They will be the first to admit that it was not easy to start with because the issues they brought up looked like criticisms.

But they persevered with their agreement to help each other, and they gradually understood that they were actually helping each other. So, this has become a regular thing and has significantly improved their relationship.

I know this concept of sharpening each other is not easy for everyone, but the goal of a Christian marriage is to please God and embody the qualities Apostle Paul talked about in 1 **Corinthians 13:4-7:** *"Love is patient, love is kind. It does not envy, it does not boast, it is not proud, it does not dishonour others, it is not self-seeking, it is not easily angered, it keeps no record of wrongs, love does not delight in evil but rejoices with the truth. It always protects, always trusts, always hopes, always perseveres".*

When couples agree to sharpen each other, it is possible for them to embody these qualities.

The process of sharpening each other allows them to talk openly, be vulnerable with each other, and be humble to receiving input so they can grow.

In other words, couples should regularly look out for each other and ensure that they are spiritual in their thinking, attitude, and how they live generally.

For this to happen, there should be questioning, encouraging, coaching and challenging each other to do the right things – living to please God first and foremost.

I am also aware of relationships where one person does not allow the 'sharpening' to take place because their personality is overpowering, and as a result, their partner feels that they do not have a voice in the relationship.

The partner who feels passive in the relationship may feel hurt by their spouse's behaviour, and if they are not able to overcome this, the relationship may not achieve its full potential.

If this describes your relationship with your spouse, what are you doing to address the situation?

I encourage you to be proactive in seeking help to resolve it for both of you.

In a relationship where the husband and wife sharpen each other, they are closer, happier, and they meet each other's emotional, spiritual and sexual needs.

In conclusion, it is inevitable that you will hurt each other because you are two individuals from different backgrounds, perhaps from different cultures. These differences may make you see things differently and may cause you to hurt each other intentionally or unintentionally.

You may be able to resolve some of the ways you hurt each other on your own, which would be great. However, where this is not possible, I advise you to give each other the permission to get help from people both of you respect and someone you know will be objective and impartial.

I hope and pray that you have taken at least one thing from this chapter that will help you to stop hurting your spouse. And when you do, and your spouse points it out to you, you will be quick and humble enough to accept and repent.

Remember, God wants to use your marriage and the pain you have gone through for his glory, and he also wishes to encourage couples who are struggling in this area of their marriage to have faith in him. If God can do it for you, he can do it for them too.

Further questions to consider:

- What are you going to do differently from now to stop hurting your spouse?

- Write your ideas down and discuss them with your spouse and children if they live with you.

Lesson Five

Unity in Marriage

Genesis 2:18-24: *18 The LORD God said, "It is not good for the man to be alone. I will make a helper suitable for him." 19 Now the LORD God had formed out of the ground all the wild animals and all the birds in the sky. He brought them to the man to see what he would name them; and whatever the man called each living creature, that was its name. 20 So the man gave names to all the livestock, the birds in the sky and all the wild animals. But for Adam no suitable helper was found. 21 So the LORD God caused the man to fall into a deep sleep; and while he was sleeping, he took one of the man's ribs and then closed up the place with flesh. 22 Then the LORD God made a woman from the rib he had taken out of the man, and he brought her to the man.*

23 The man said, "This is now bone of my bones and flesh of my flesh; she shall be called 'woman,' for she was taken out of man." 24 That is why a man leaves his father and mother and is united to his wife, and they become one flesh.

Question:

How can you and your spouse operate in a way where you are one in everything you do?

It was God's plan from the beginning that married COUPLES ARE UNITED as one flesh, so it is critical for a relationship to function as God intends it. Therefore, married couples _must_ strive for unity – no matter what. A married man is incomplete without his wife and likewise, a married woman is incomplete without her husband.

The bond between them must be so strong that they become inseparable. I like the fact that in the culture I grew up, when you see a married couple at a social gathering, you will easily recognise them because the attire they wear are cut from the same material.

God's plan for man:

It is **not good** for man to be alone; I will make a helper **suitable** for him.

Of all God's creation at the time, the only thing that was not good was man being alone. Hence, God saw it fit to make a helper suitable for him.

Perhaps because of the challenges you may be going through with your spouse at the moment, it is hard to believe that God has put you together or you are suitable for each other.

You may be saying to yourself, "if my spouse is suitable for me, why are we always at loggerheads most of the time?"

In my work with couples over the years, I have come to believe that when couples surrender their wills to God's will, they begin to see great improvements in themselves as individuals, and this coincidentally produces a massive improvement in their marriage.

This phenomenon will become true for both of you if you decide to do marriage God's way rather than your way.

I pray that as you read this chapter and do the exercises, you and your spouse will see the adjustments both of you need to make in your marriage to get back to believing that you are suitable for each other.

I encourage you to start seeing your spouse beyond the challenges you are having right now and see them for what they could become.

In Genesis 2:19, God paraded all the animals he had created for man to name them and the Bible tells us that whatever name the man gave them, that was their name.

None of them were the BONE of HIS BONES and FLESH of HIS FLESH. (Husbands, are we not happy that Adam did not choose any of the animals as his companion?)

When Adam woke up and saw the person next to him in verse 23, you could just imagine the joy and delight in his heart. You can appreciate why he said, "*this is now BONE of MY BONES and FLESH of MY FLESH, so she shall be called a WOMAN*".

Denoting someone who is a mirror image of himself, someone **like him** *and yet* **different**.

Physiologically, a man and a woman are different, but when it comes to having the attributes of God (patience, kindness, goodness, love, forgiveness, caring; to mention but a few) they can be alike. The presence of these attributes in a marriage helps couples to strive for unity, the oneness God intends, and makes the marriage a joy. Conversely, the absence of these attributes in a marriage causes disunity and makes it a burden.

Choose what type of marriage you want for yourself today!

Steps to having unity in your marriage.

The first and most important step to take in having unity in your marriage is to seek unity with Christ before seeking it with each other.

UNITY WITH CHRIST

The picture below tells the story perfectly well. We should aim to do things in the right order, seek unity with Christ first before unity with your spouse.

So, be warned, don't put the cart before the horse.

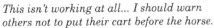

This isn't working at all... I should warn others not to put their cart before the horse.

For the majority of the couples we see during marriage coaching sessions, they want unity with their spouse at the expense of unity with Christ first, which is bonkers! Yet, as much as my wife and I try our best to encourage them not to think this way, some find it hard to change their mind, and as a result, they never change and the issue causing them unhappiness in their marriage persists.

God has arranged things in a certain order because he is the creator and he wants us to follow his plan for our marriage to work out well for us.

You do not dig up oranges from the ground, you pluck them from the tree. On the contrary, you don't pluck potatoes from trees, you dig them from the ground. If you see your neighbour digging for oranges, you would be worried about them. Why? Because they are not following the right order of things. Similarly, I am worried about couples who want a great marriage but are not seeking unity with Christ first.

So, get a grip, and make a commitment to put the horse before the cart – seek unity with Christ first and foremost, and by doing so, you will attain the unity God wants for you and your spouse.

In the UK where I have lived for a number of years, the weather is freezing in the winter months, so the heaters or fireplaces are turned on to warm the house up.

The closer one is to the heater or fireplace, the warmer one feels. Likewise, the farther away someone is, the colder they are. If this analogy is applied to being close to God, the closer we are to God, the more we will embrace His qualities (love, kindness, goodness, forgiveness, grace, sacrifice; etc) in our marriage.

The diagram below shows how important it is for couples to make the effort to move closer to God simultaneously and not just one person making the effort.

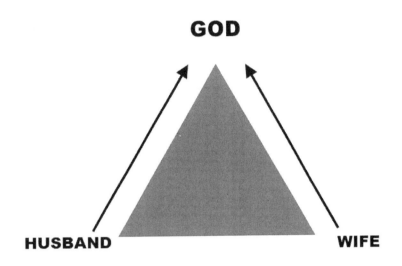

Four observations I would like to highlight from this diagram:

1. If one of you is growing closer to God while the other person remains at the lowest point of the triangle, the distance between you increases.

2. It is better for both of you to make the decision to draw closer to God to improve the closeness between you.

3. You should not depend on your spouse to get closer to God, it is an individual decision. When both of you have

made the decision to draw closer to God, you can spur each other on to live this way.

4.   The closer both of you are to God, the smaller the gap between you spiritually, and the closer you will be to each other.

Please study the following scriptures to see the importance of seeking God first:

- **Matthew 6:33:** *"Seek first his kingdom and its righteousness and all these things will be given to you as well".*

- **2 Corinthians 8:5:** *"And they exceeded our expectations: they gave themselves first of all to the Lord, and then by the will of God also to us".*

- **Proverbs 3:5-6:** *Trust in the Lord with all your heart and lean not on your own understanding; in all your ways submit to Him, and He will make your paths straight".*

The key to having a great marriage is to give yourself fully to the Lord.

To give yourself fully to the Lord means:

- You need to trust Him in both good and bad, especially when you face challenges that rock your world.

- You don't waiver in your trust in God because He will always work things out for your good in the end.

- You make Him a priority in your life and He will take care of all that concerns you.

- Submit your will to Him and He will straighten your paths.

I know the above points may be challenging for some people when they are going through a rough patch in life; they may even question the existence of God. They may be asking themselves, "why me? Of all the people in the world, why do I have to be the one in this precarious and challenging position?"

There have been times in my life when I have questioned the existence of God in various situations, especially at work, when I felt unfairly treated.

In 2003-2004, I worked for a housing association that manages services that supports older people. I worked over 50 hours a week (my contracted hours were 36) to ensure that the service ran well and to save money for this organisation. However, an unfortunate incident occurred while I was off work and I received the blame. This situation put a lot of stress on me and as a result, I developed high blood pressure. This was a low point in my life, but in the end, all I could do was to put my trust in God; He created me and knows what is best for me. I read about Joseph in Genesis (Chapter 37, 39 to 45), and it gave me a lift to trust that God would work things out in the end. Fortunately, God did work things out for me. In 2005, he presented me with a much better job.

Similarly, no matter how challenging your situation is, aim for unity with Christ and all will be well with you and your spouse. He is the third person in your relationship, so put His words into practise, and you will see a difference in your life and in your marriage.

Unity with your spouse:

What should this unity with your spouse look like? How would you know when you have reached the point of unity?

If you have seen pictures or read stories about Siamese or conjoined twins, you will know that they are inseparable. Some of them share the same heart, and limbs, and others are joined at the hip or head. The connection and closeness they have is remarkable, and the closeness and connections between you and your spouse should be remarkable too.

Your spouse should be:

- Your best friend.
- Your confidant.
- Your soulmate.
- Your supporter.

If you do not have this type of relationship with your spouse, please don't despair because there is hope and room to work on your relationship. God considers us all a work in progress; He is the potter and we are the clay, wanting to mould us into his image *(Isaiah 64:8)*.

STEPS TO DEVELOPING UNITY WITH YOUR SPOUSE

VULNERABILITY: According to Brené Brown in the "Power of Vulnerability", vulnerability is the *POWER TO BE SEEN*. She also stresses that the key to human connection is vulnerability.

Until you and your spouse see each other for who you really are; your quirks, emotions, and how your past is affecting you now, it will be difficult to be fully connected.

It is ironic that what couples need to do to form unity with their spouse is often what they don't want to do.

Most married couple who are serious about their relationship want to feel connected to their spouse, but some find it difficult to be vulnerable and would rather not reveal the hidden part of their life.

One of the most transforming talks Helen and I had in the early days of our marriage was when she told me she was sexually abused as a child. I had wondered why she was always uneasy about the physical side of our relationship, but I never pried.

I admired her for having the courage to be vulnerable and talk about it. Letting me into this sad incident in her past brought us closer. We talked about how to manage the physical side of our relationship going forward, and as a result, she felt free and liberated. She later said that she did not know how to bring it up with me, but she knew she had to pick up the courage to talk about it.

Vulnerability is also about being open with your fears or letting your guard down.

To enhance your relationship with your spouse, letting your guard down is an invitation to open your heart to your spouse, which is an amazing time to bond with each other.

Doing this helps your spouse know you better and may help to release tension in your marriage.

Take the case of Soji and Elaine: they have been together for 35 years and have been married for 25 years. They have 3 grown up children and 3 grandchildren. Throughout their relationship, Elaine has always felt that Soji has never shown any sympathy or understanding when she brings up issues of great concerns to him. He has always been dismissive of her concerns and appeared uninterested. He saw them as negatives and he abhors negative people.

Even when Elaine was diagnosed with terminal illness, she tried to let him know how the illness was affecting her on several occasions, he did not show any empathy or interest to understand how she was feeling. Elaine sought the advice of a mutual friend they both respected and stated her concern about Soji's behaviour.

This friend asked for a private audience with Soji and made him realise how his lack of sympathy for Elaine's situation was unloving, and how it makes her feel disconnected from him.

For the first time, the penny dropped and he realised how aloof he had been. He arranged for both of them to go away for a weekend, which is when he finally listened to her and apologised for his behaviour with tears running down his cheeks.

He said he had been in denial because he did not want to show the vulnerable side of his character and let his guard down. He said that his upbringing of "never show your emotions to people, they will consider you weak" has formed his character and behaviour.

Needless to say, Elaine was excited about the outcome of the conversation and said, "that was all I have been asking for" - to be understood and cared about.

However, he was broken and felt like he should have done this earlier rather than keeping his guard up.

Some people are guarded because they have been hurt in the past or due to the way they were raised, but letting your guard down could be the most powerful thing you do; it allows your spouse to know you for who you really are.

When you let your guard down, you feel free, like a weight has been lifted off your shoulders.

Your life should be an open book to each other. If your spouse asks you a question about your life, please tell them the truth. If you are afraid to tell them the truth because of fear of reprisal, you need to get help. In **1 John 4 v 18**, *"There is no fear in love. But perfect love drives out fear, because fear has to do with punishment. The one who fears in not made perfect in love"*.

This passage of scripture is self-explanatory; there should be no fear in love. If you really love each other, you should not be afraid to raise issues with each other that affects your happiness in the marriage.

When we accept vulnerability, we become kinder, empathetic and understanding of each other.

Vulnerability makes you beautiful to your spouse. Vulnerability may have the connotation of inadequacy – which is how people with a circular mindset understand vulnerability. They see a vulnerable person as weak and most people do not want to be associated with weakness.

So, they pretend that they are strong and present themselves in this way to outsiders and even to their spouse. However, doing this is wrong. The Christian's perspective on vulnerability emphasises that God's power is made perfect in our weaknesses.

2 Corinthians 12:9: *"But He said to me, "My grace is sufficient for you, for my power is made perfect in weakness." Therefore, I will boast all the more gladly of my weaknesses, so that the power of Christ may rest upon me. For the sake of Christ, then, I am content with weaknesses, insults, hardships, persecutions, and calamities. For when I am weak, then I am strong."*

The above passage of scripture encourages my heart and gives me a better understanding of the importance of vulnerability in my marriage and in my life. It makes me truly believe that God's power is made perfect in me when I am vulnerable, so I can become strong. This is the opposite of circular thinking. In my interactions with couples, those who approach each other from a position of vulnerability seem to have a better relationship than those who approach each other from a position of strength – with circular mind-set.

Jesus showed us the example we should follow when he was in the Garden of Gethsemane: **Mark 14:34-35:** *"My soul is overwhelmed with sorrow to the point of death,"* he said to his disciples. *"Stay here and keep watch."* Going a little farther, he fell to the ground and prayed that if it is possible, the hour might pass from him. "Abba Father," he said; everything is possible for you. Take this cup from me. Yet not what I will, but what you will."

He submitted his will to God and asked for God's will to be done.

What an amazing example of vulnerability for us to follow. Sometimes, I want my will, my comfort, and self-preservation rather than allowing God's will to be done.

Revealing your deepest thoughts and feelings to your spouse (being vulnerable) should help to draw you closer and become more united.

Apostle Paul was another example of a vulnerable man, so let us learn the benefits of vulnerability from Paul; his openness and transparency like when he mentions persecuting the church *(Galatians 1:13)*. He also speaks of his own weaknesses or vulnerabilities, but he realised and taught that God's power is made perfect in our "weakness".

In fact, Paul is the strongest at the same time he is the weakest. How is that possible? It's possible due to "the power of Christ" that rests upon him.

When you share your weaknesses with your spouse and they share theirs with you, it gives you a platform to build your relationship on and help each other to overcome those weaknesses and turn them into strengths.

Further questions to consider:

- How vulnerable are you about sharing your past?

- Does your spouse really know the things that make you feel secure / insecure?

- Are you open about your weaknesses? If not, what is holding you back?

- Are you worried about whether your spouse would have married you if they knew what they now know about you?

Please remember that vulnerability is good for your relationship because it shows your heart and draws you and your spouse closer to one another. It has worked for me in my relationship with my wife and for countless couples we have worked with. If you commit to being really vulnerable, you will see the benefits individually and the positive effect it will have on your marriage. So, please don't delay any longer.

If you find this aspect of your life a challenge, I suggest that you get help from a mature couple you know, or get advice from someone more knowledgeable in this area; for example, a marriage coach.

TOGETHERNESS

The Oxford Dictionary defines togetherness as "The happy feeling you have when you are with people you like, especially family and friends".

To have this happy feeling of being together with your spouse, I encourage you to look beyond your own needs and think of how best to meet your spouse's needs.

Please see the passage of scripture below that summarises this succinctly for me:

Philippians 2:1-4: *"Therefore, if you have any encouragement from being united with Christ, if any comfort from his love, if any common sharing in the Spirit, if any tenderness and compassion, 2 then make my joy complete by being like-minded, having the same love, being one in spirit and of one mind. 3 Do nothing out of selfish ambition or vain conceit. Rather, in humility value others above yourselves, 4 not looking to your own interests but each of you to the interests of the others."*

I particularly like this passage as an individual, and my wife and I use it a lot in our marriage coaching sessions with our clients. It presents married couples with the template for togetherness; the spirit of being in the relationship to help each other to be the best version of themselves.

What will your relationship look like if you and your spouse are:

- Like-minded?
- Have the same love for each other?
- Be of one spirit?
- Do nothing out of selfish ambition or vain conceit?
- In humility, value each other above yourselves?
- Not looking for your own interests but for the interests of your spouse?

Wow! You might be thinking to yourself, is this type of relationship possible? YES, it is possible when you and your spouse agree to put the biblical principles and the teachings of Christ into practice; they will help you to draw closer to God together, and consequently, to each other.

Please note that being of the same mind does not mean that you agree with each other on everything. In my travels, when I see couples who are in their twilight years and have been married for over 50 years, I like to ask them the secret of their long-married life together. I will never forget the answer this couple gave me; they have been married for over 60 years.

He said, "Just say yes to everything and you will avoid being in trouble with her" - that's how they have managed their relationship. I asked him whether that meant he genuinely agrees with everything his wife suggests, and he said no, but to keep the peace, he had to say yes to everything. That kind of marriage does not allow him the freedom to express his opinion.

Suffice it to say that when there is an issue to be discussed, you must have the freedom to express your opinion and settle for a course of action that you are both happy with. And to get to this point, both of you have to do what it says in **Philippians 2:1** – 'being united with Christ' will help you to aim for and achieve togetherness in your marriage.

Further questions and statements to consider:

- Compare and contrast your life as a married person to when you were single. Discuss your findings with your spouse.

- Describe ways you can serve your spouse by looking out for his or her interests above your own?

- Do you find yourself responding with anger when your agenda is challenged? If yes, explore the reasons why you get angry, and get help to resolve them.

- Describe your first, unfiltered response when your spouse wrongs you?

- How is wanting things done your way without respect for your spouse's preferences affecting the unity between you?

Final words from me:

It has been a pleasure to be able to share my life, my marriage and the experiences I have acquired as a marriage coach, with you in the five lessons you have read.

Here are a couple of questions to take away with you:

What are the things that resonates with you?

What are you going to do differently to boost your marriage?

The things that stood out for me in writing this book are:

- The benefits of applying biblical principles to my marriage.

- Vulnerability is key to having a close relationship with my wife.

- The need to give my wife a voice, so we can help sharpen each other. As a result, be a better version of ourselves.

- The need to be clear when communicating with my wife. Understanding that she is not a mind reader. Putting her in this position could frustrate her.

- Striving for unity with God first, which will naturally lead to unity with my wife.

- Taking responsibility to change my heart, irrespective of how my wife is doing.

- Understanding that my response to the scriptures has an impact on my life as a person and on my marriage.

I would like to assure you that, no matter the state of your marriage right now or how long you have been married for, whether you are unhappy in your marriage or having an okay marriage, if you make the decision today to apply the biblical principles outlined in this book to your life, they will transform your marriage for the better.

God wants you to have a great and fulfilling marriage. You cannot do marriage your way or the Hollywood way, you have to do it God's way to enjoy it.

Whatever resonates with you from these lessons, I urge you to put them into practise, so do not delay. May the peace of God be with you. Amen.

I would like to hear your stories: please send them to: *info@marriagesupport.org.uk*

You can scan this QR code with your phone to send the email now:

REFERENCES

Lesson One

"The Surprising Benefits of Kissing" published in Psychology today in 2012, Sean Horan

Lesson Two

The Spotlight Effect and the Illusion of Transparency: Egocentric Assessments of How We Are Seen by Others, Thomas Gilovich and Kenneth Savitsky, 1999

The term "Illusion of Transparency" was coined in 1998 by Gilovich, Saitsky, and Medvec in their research paper. Their research showed that we tend to overestimate the degree our thoughts or emotions "leak out" and become known to those observing us.

Psychology Today February 2019 – 9 Signs You Might be a Cognitive Miser by Aditi Mehra

Lesson Three

Rick Hanson: Don't Quarrel – Psychology Today, February 2013

Boundaries in Marriage – Dr Henry Cloud & Dr John Townsend.

Lesson Four

Hurt Feelings in Couple Relationships: Towards Integrative Models of the Negative Effect of Hurtful Events. By Judith Feeney. First Published August 1, 2004-Sage Journals

Laura K. Guerrero, Coping with Hurtful Events, February 2012, Communication Current Essay, Arizona State University.

Lesson Five

Brené Brown 'Power of Vulnerability'.

Printed in Great Britain
by Amazon